23634

Universities and Research

Universities and Research

Observations on the United States and Sweden

by Gunnar Boalt, University of Stockholm

Herman Lantz, Southern Illinois University

Wiley Interscience Division
John Wiley & Sons, Inc.   New York, London, Sydney

© *Gunnar Boalt & Herman Lantz*

Almqvist & Wiksell Förlag AB

Stockholm 1970

Library of Congress Catalog Card Number 72-114718

Printed in Sweden by

Almqvist & Wiksells Boktryckeri AB

Uppsala 1970

Contents

CHAPTER 1

The Academic Man in America

Although sociologists have been hard at work studying almost every facet of social organization, they have largely ignored the academic man and the constellation in which he functions in the university. Apart from the efforts of such persons as Logan Wilson, Ted Caplow, and Reece McGee, there has been relatively little effort to understand the academic man, the structure in which he functions, and the consequences of the adaptations and adjustments that he makes. Such lack of systematic study may in part result from an unwillingness of sociologists to study a phenomenon so very close to oneself; perhaps even a fear of facing and examining the plight in which one is implicated. Finally, there may be a concern that one not offend colleagues or the administrations of academic institutions. Nevertheless, for whatever reason, or combination of reasons, the subject has been largely ignored.

The purpose of the present presentation is to explore the plight of the academic man comparatively in the United States and Sweden to see what they have in common, and to understand the basis of their plight. While the analysis draws observations from the experience of sociologists, the basic views expressed should be of considerable import for academic persons in all fields.

The title of this chapter suggests a plight, indeed, a dilemma. In order to understand the context in which the plight takes place the following oversimplified theoretical formulations may be stated.

(1) The academic man in America operates in a status hierarchy, such a hierarchy represents a distribution of values ranging from high to low.
(2) Rank represents one such status differential, ranging from instructor to full professor.
(3) Within each status level there are the respective roles of researcher and teacher, or some combination of the two. While there are exceptions, teaching as an exclusive or primary role is subordinate in value to the role of researcher-writer. Although the researcher-writer role carries with

it teaching responsibility, it is usually limited and is not the basis of the individual's academic status.

(4) The academic man pursues roles and goals commensurate with receiving maximum benefits.

(5) Role conflict arises when teaching is personally and professionally unrewarding and when the pursuit of a research career becomes unfeasible, or when teaching is personally rewarding but professionally unrewarding. Under these conditions new role adaptations with the university structure are considered.

As a first step in this analysis it is necessary to deal in detail with some of the dimensions of the educational structure in America and the values and goals in which it is implicated.

The Role of Teaching

Whatever arguments may be advanced about the need and importance of good teaching, it fails by and large to carry the status it may well deserve. A chairman of an academic department of one of America's leading universities made the following remark to a group of graduate students: "Do the best job of teaching you can, but it is my impression that few people have been rewarded for good teaching, and I can't think of anybody who was ever fired for being a poor teacher!" This assertion, if true, represents an indication of the relative importance placed on the teaching role. Although many American institutions are currently going through a reexamination of their teaching effort, it is difficult to tell how long the desire to stress teaching will continue. Even efforts to reward good teaching, perhaps motivated by administrative guilt, or a short range response to concern about students, are likely to be limited, soon giving way to be emphasis on research and writing. The status differential between the role of teacher and the role of researcher-writer, along with commensurate rewards, must be seen within the context of a more encompassing scheme of values from within the university and the society. An understanding of the sometimes complex and intricate series of institutional arrangements in which the modern university in American Society is implicated in may enable us to understand the basis of conflicts that beset the academic man. It is important at the outset to ask why there is a status differential between the two roles, teacher and research-writer. Why the emphasis on research and writing?

8

The Significance of Research and Writing in the University Enterprise

Apart from the fact that there are concerns for the university's traditional role regarding scientific and scholarly investigations, there are more *instrumental* considerations that have to be noted.

Here one must understand particular aspects of the broader American value system of which the modern American University is a part. A first factor has to do with size. Generally speaking, larger institutions and efforts carry with them greater *prestige, power,* and *importance,* demand greater budgets, and wield influence, albeit that some small select universities may also possess influence. The fact that an increase in numbers of students ready for college is present facilitates the university's argument for growth and expansion.

A second significant factor in addition to prestige, power, and influence, is the pursuit of the American ideal of *individualism.* Individualism is the basis of the persistent and herculean efforts university administrators make in the face of tradition to move from small, insignificant normal schools to major institutions; a fact which can be documented repeatedly.

These efforts often originate as boot strap-grass roots operations, involving one or two significant administrators with leadership, who bring along a faculty, an area committed to mass education, and its political figures, so that vital ongoing support is forthcoming. Such shifts in the status of institutions is facilitated by the fact that administrators in such a role find opportunities for personal reward particularly good, since administrators today come upon the scene at a time when the opportunities favorable to expansion and growth in America are pronounced. American Higher Education offers one of the most important and significant opportunities for status mobility, especially for those who are implicated in its structure. This combination of men actively seeking mobility within a social context which permits and favors mobility facilitates change and growth of the university significantly.

Egalitarianism is the third significant factor for understanding university growth, since many university administrations have come to feel that with appropriate effort and public support they can become equal to *major institutions.* The fact that American society has for some time been committed to the support of higher education for the youth of the nation has aided this trend.

When we speak of growth and influence, we are thinking largely in terms of graduate education. Few schools aspire to become outstanding undergraduate institutions; and any commitment to do so may be tenuous and dependent largely on the administrative views of those in control. Changes in administrative leadership may bring with them drastic changes in orientation. For example, many faculty have devoted their careers to stressing good teaching since such views were at one point in time consistent with those held by the administration. Nevertheless, administrators may change more often in the direction of adopting the universalistic norms of research and writing, particularly in the move from the teacher training normal school to the university. It is precisely this change that creates considerable anxiety in faculty who, after many years with relatively good salaries but commitments to undergraduate teaching, find themselves being pushed to change their professional orientations from teaching to writing and research. Such individuals after many years of service may find themselves unable to remain at the institution with any sense of comfort, and unable to move to a position that pays as well due to the relatively high salaries they have accumulated over the years. Those who stay on in their positions very frequently become the basis for a core of bitter and resentful faculty.

Growth, Individualism, and Egalitarianism

The significance of particular types of growth and the search for power, prestige, individualism, and egalitarianism are therefore significant values to which Americans subscribe; and it is the prominent place which these values hold which must be understood in examining the importance of the *researcher-writer role.*

Thus, once an administrative hierarchy of a small, and perhaps intellectually insignificant, institution develops aspirations, a set of forces are put into operation which make certain consequences inevitable. The search for talented professionals is on, the individual with stature in his field. Mostly there emerges the concern for *research and writing,* since these activities focus attention on the university, and bring with it publicity and interest from the public. Finally, they facilitate the possibility of graduate education since funds from research become a means of facilitating the increase of graduate enrollments. It would be a mistake, however, to attribute administrative support for research only to needs for an expanded graduate program. Certainly such interest also stems from the view that vital graduate education is intimately tied to ongoing research activity. In terms of such a view one who is not so engaged is both a bad model and an ineffective teacher. In addition, high productivity in the perspective of research and writing is considered the mark of a good university, and by and large all universities interested in growth accept these values. In one instance it is reliably reported that a university was willing to place a new staff member on leave with full pay (not a sabbatical) in order that he finish a book which would carry the new university's name. While there are those universities who defiantly declare that they will not become implicated in placing undue stress on productivity, it is probable that those universities mainly express an attitude of "sour grapes" rather than wholehearted conviction. They are for the most part those who cloak themselves with the garment of austerity making a virtue of it, but basically feeling much left out of the mainstream of ongoing university intellectual activity.

What are the implications of our remarks? With respect to the university itself, our remarks suggest that once a university decides on a particular pattern of growth it commits itself to a differential set of values and rewards for the teacher and the researcher-writer, irrespective of the pronouncements the university makes in regard to teaching. Even if a particular university were willing to commit itself to the permanent reward of good teching, whatever that may be, the rewards for research and writing in most American universities would still be greater.

Thus, the university creates a set of inconsistencies and dilemmas for itself. In addition, it creates a set of structures to implement research and writing which may become complex and difficult to control, a special problem to be dealt with.

In the course of evolving a policy for the growth of the university, the administration and the faculty embark upon patterns of dealing with one another that create an ever complicated series of problems.

In turning our attention to the academic man himself we note that the status differentials we have described indicate that the academic man in America is socialized in a dual value system; each set of values conflicting with the other. On the one hand he expects to earn a livelihood for the most part by teaching, a noble and honorable profession which contributes to the youth of the nation. Nevertheless, he also learns that this activity will bring minimal rewards from a university administration. Moreover, teaching will do little to enhance his professional status. Pressures appear from all quarters cloaked in various ways. Faculty working in their own way, even good teachers performing well, continuously may find their work upset by suggestions that they should be doing something

11

else. In some instances the shaking of a complacent faculty is necessary, but often it results in people abandoning what they can best do in favor of something they do less well. Many under these circumstances end up as poor researchers and writers. Their teaching may well suffer as well because energies are depleted by other tasks; and because the individual may find the role of writer-researcher personally unsatisfactory. The situation is replete with conflict at best.

CHAPTER 2

University Growth and Research Policy

We have already sketched some of the implications for the university once it embarks upon a pattern of emphasis on research and writing. In order to implement the many functions which research and writing are to perform it becomes necessary to generate a good sized bureaucratic organization an Office of Research and Projects, to assist with dissemination, of knowledge about where research grants may be obtained, the requirements of the agency, the processing of research applications. Such a structure may also assist the individual with minimal university funds to get underway so that he may be in a position to apply for a larger grant at a later time.

Sometimes the organization involves a senior administrative official, a vice-president or director in charge of research and projects, with a large staff to handle the administrative details associated with a research and projects program. One of the major tasks which such an organization has is the attraction of *research contracts and grants.* In fact the stature of the organization and its director are in direct proportion to the amount of outside research and grant money brought in.

Implications for the University and Its Faculty

The implications of these structures, designed to facilitate research projects and ultimately writing, may be noted as follows.

(1) The very creation of the structure represents a university commitment to research; and the continuation of the structure necessitates a commitment from faculty to engage in research. Thus, the existence of the structure is a reminder for the faculty of their obligation to the university.

(2) Such agencies may *influence research policy* by seeking out funding agencies and appropriate faculty to engage in research. As such they

can come perilously close to directing what scholars will research and the methods they will employ, especially when it is known what granting agencies will require in the way of problem and method. With the advent of grantsmanship (competence in preparation of research proposals) the university research and projects agency may take over large areas of preparing the research proposal, especially the design. The more inadequate faculty member may, indeed, give up this basic obligation and responsibility; a tendency which has serious implications for him and for his profession.

(3) Such local research structures are also significant since they take on bureaucratic characteristics by efforts to grow and expand, assuming ever increasing functions as previously noted; and the university may be willing to encourage growth since they can facilitate the attraction of vast sums of money.

(4) In the pursuit of funds for research and projects there is the very real danger that the outside funding agency requirements and interests may not be carefully examined and evaluated. Basic ethical and moral concerns about what the research seeks, for which interest groups, the net effect or impact of research can become irrelevant. It is this single fact which may be the most significant in understanding recent criticisms and concerns about the scholar's and university's responsibility in research; particularly when such research may reflect involvement in the internal affairs of another society. The drift to seeking large scale funding for what may be deemed dubious and immoral projects may be less the result of a conspiracy between the university and federal granting agencies; and primarily the results of what may be an essentially *amoral bureaucratic university research structure ever in search of funds, without constraining influence and guidance from the administration and its faculty.*

(5) In addition, the overall university setting we have discussed results in a compulsive need to engage in research. Problems are desperately sought after, especially problems that can attract financial support. Academic departments so inclined can soon find themselves with an acute phase of *projectitis,* frantically searching for research grants for the purpose of bringing in funds. Many of the problems cannot be researched, others can but may contribute little theoretically, methodologically, or substantively. There may be nothing more demoralizing to the researcher and the student undergoing training than the endless, ritualistic grinding out of meaningless research along with meaningless reports.

(6) A sixth significant implication in the present discussion has to do

14

with the fact that research grants bring with them prestige and power for individuals and groups of faculty. The size of many grants runs up into hundreds of thousands of dollars. They place the faculty member so involved in a position of unusual power and importance. He is in a position to make many demands and to *blackmail the administration with threats to leave.*

It must be pointed out, however, that such a state of affairs could hardly arise had university administrators not fostered and created the necessary climate in at least two ways. It is in part a result of their willingness to absorb without careful examination the values associated with growth, the search for power and prestige, and the emphasis on research and writing. It is also part of the price they have to pay for their involvement.

In addition, university administrations have traditionally operated in a situation in which desirable faculty were in great supply. This has meant that administrations were free to pay as little as possible while imposing heavy teaching and committee responsibilities. Many faculty who came through such a period in American Higher Education, and the Ph.D.'s they trained, are familiar with this history and are now inclined *to extract as much as they can in return,* feeling that university administrations left to their own devices would return to the norms of a scarcity economy, minimizing rewards. This view complicates the bargaining process; and many administrators unaware of the past history find the agressive behavior of faculty difficult to understand.

Student Rebellion

Recent problems with students on the American college campus have been identified as arising out of professorial over involvement with research; such over involvement presumably leads to disinterest in the student and the neglect of teaching. Insofar as such an accusation is correct the over involvement has to be seen in light of our total discussion. It seems less than reasonable to many faculty to expect them to give "their all" to a responsibility which the university does not value greatly which will reduce their mobility and bring few personal rewards. (7) A seventh significant implication has to do with the freedom of the university which is invariably in danger of becoming compromised. First, by having its research policy directed and controlled by granting agencies with the local office of research and projects a minor representative. Second, by being put into a position of vulnerability with respect to their capacity to criticize federal and state funding agencies.

How free is an academic department or university dependent on the federal or state government for major support to criticize the policies of federal granting agencies who make unreasonable demands on the researcher? What are the consequences when support from funding agencies is withdrawn?

CHAPTER 3

Adaptations

Virtually all academic people in American universities attempt to come to terms with the problems we outlined previously. These are persistent dilemmas and contradictions. Searching for a position of significance in his work, the academic man finds himself caught in conflict between the role of teacher, a role of relatively low status, and the role of researcher and writer, a role of high status but hazardous and replete with burdens and difficulties. There are those who initially pursue the role of the teacher. Such a role may be satisfactory for a while, but is likely to turn sour when rewards are not forthcoming. Some of these individuals feel trapped by the system that tells them one thing but really means another. They may gravitate toward smaller or lesser known institutions where pressures to engage in research and writing will not be forthcoming. They may remain at larger institutions but be poorly paid, very slowly advanced, and sometimes the object of scorn and ridicule by their colleagues. As a group they become a core of resentful people at war with their institutions and colleagues, resenting changes which accent their plight, for feeling rejected. They complain about universities not fulfilling their function, abandoning students, and settling for false values. They are not altogether wrong, but much of what they see is a function of feeling out of place due to being rejected by the larger community of scholars.

Another academic group may become research oriented; they accept the values, the means, and the goals. Yet there are hazards involved.

To engage in research today means almost super human effort. It involves keeping up with a vast amount of literature which is ever growing. Not only is it no longer possible to keep up with an academic field, it is no longer possible to keep up with a field of specialization since there are specialities within specialities. This means tremendous amounts of time in the development of research designs, proposals, and the need to contact foundations and agencies. If one is fortunate enough to receive a grant, there are pressures to produce results. This in itself can be quite unpredictable since results may not be published for a variety of reasons. There may be some fault with the method; it may be the results are inconclusive; it may be that someone else has published something very similar.

Others, on the other hand, are unable to apply for grants, many are turned down. Those who receive grants may be unable to complete the project, or even organize their results in publishable form. The role requires tremendous dedication and discipline. The conflicts may become quite intense.

Administrative Roles

Thus, there are many individuals who find both the role of teacher, or of researcher-writer unsatisfactory and unrewarding. How do such persons deal with the desire for positions of importance and status within the university setting, without the means to do so? *The administrative role, ranging from chairman up to dean, vice-president, and president, along with directorships of university agencies, is one which can satisfy many of the requirements for status and prestige in the university community without pressures to engage in research and writing.* It is thus a role which attracts large numbers of faculty caught in the type of role conflict we have described.

Such faculty may have the best of all possible worlds. They possess legitimate power over others, over scholars, their salaries, promotions, and working conditions. Yet they are not called upon to engage in research and writing since their time is absorbed with other activities. They speak of the terrible ordeal of their work and they speak of the "wonderful life of the professor" who can do what he enjoys most. Yet to an administrative role that they profess not to enjoy they devote many years of their lives. Few resign, many leave only when forced to do so.

The rapid creation and expansion of many administrative roles has been a safety valve for the pressures that beset the academic man in America. It has enabled the old slogan of "publish or perish" to become obsolete. Nevertheless, it may be that administrators who have moved into administration in search of power or prestige, not attainable in other academic roles, never really resolve the dilemma. One finds these people moving in and out of administration; frequently apologies for not being able to engage in writing and research are forthcoming. University administrations have an ample supply of available talent from the large corps of teachers and researchers who have selected themselves out of their respective roles, or who have been selected out for one reason or another. The administrative role filled by these types represents in some sense a welcome development for those administrations in institutions that look upon themselves as essentially watchdogs of public interests. Such administrations are most likely, although not exclusively, to be located in institutions moving from a small school status to a large school status where all deans and chairmen are not in full accord with the patterns of growth. There is the need to see that taxpayers' money is properly spent, faculty have to make a strict accounting of how time is spent and teaching loads have to be at a maximum. What appears as a concern for the public interest is often anti-intellectualism and hostility to change. These administrators sense a kindred spirit with faculty who have been selected out or who select themselves out of research and writing. These are the kinds of people most likely to internalize the administrative point of view; they may become spokesmen for the administration; and many of those who select administration for the reasons suggested may become the most oppressive administrators, those who enforce bureaucratic norms without question.

Since university administrations operate with the norms of a scarcity economy; resources are limited. There is always a need to enforce the norms of austerity which are unpopular; and there is need for a particular mental set to invoke such norms, that is a mental set which combines unresolved hostility toward the academic man and thorough internalization of the norms of the administration. The fact that such individuals exist helps perpetuate certain kinds of administrative systems.

Insofar as faculty choose administration as an escape from the pressures to produce, on the one hand, and what they may define as academic obscurity on the other hand (teaching), they are vulnerable to the manipulation of those above them. For the longer they remove themselves from the research and writing role, the more difficult and painful it becomes to return to such a role. Given such needs, it becomes easy to understand how such administrators deal with basic academic problems on an essentially political basis, with each administrator primarily concerned about the reactions of those groups on which his support is dependent. A president must please the vice-presidents; a vice-president must please both the president and the deans. A dean worries about the vice-president and the chairmen. The chairman has to please the dean and the important groups in his department.

The only recourse open to the administrator who does not like his position is to move to other administrative positions in the hope that these will be better or return to teaching at a reduced salary, a difficult choice. Often they are trapped in a web of their own making and find it difficult to act, to move, or to change.

Having made these points, it is necessary to make the following qualifying comments:

(1) The remarks represent no general indictment of administrative roles. University administrations perform vital and necessary tasks and, in the best sense, are leaders of the academic community.

(2) Not all who enter administration do so because of a need for power and prestige, not readily found in another role. No one can ascertain the number that do.

(3) Many of those who enter administration because prestige and commensurate rewards in other roles was not forthcoming do not necessarily respond by efforts to control scholars and researchers. Even those who may have entered administration in order to escape conflicts in other roles very frequently transcend their own impulses and rise to unexpected heights. In this regard, many who would have been mediocre at research and writing find a role which is personally rewarding and socially productive. The best of this group identify with total institutional needs, including those of the faculty, and find a significant and constructive role for themselves.

Recruitment for Administration

How do faculty members interested in administration make themselves available? Professor Boalt in some of his writing suggests that those who engage in the hazards of research go through an evaluation of strategies and alternatives should research and writing become disappointing. One such alternative is to place greater weight and emphasis on some other, perhaps non-research, role as a compensation. If we apply this view to the present discussion, we can suggest that some researchers in view of the special difficulties associated with research and writing probably entertain alternate moves, such as the move into administration, at many points in their careers. For some the administrative role may have appeal before research has been undertaken. For others the interest may arise after initial failures to produce research or publish; for still others at a later stage. Thus, the process of considering administration or other alternatives is probably a constant ongoing activity, conscious or unconscious, and it probably sets into operation a series of steps which are designed to enhance the chances of being tapped for the administrative role. Interestingly enough the fact that many faculty claim surprise when they are called upon for service in an administrative role may be less a surprise to those who have observed their daily behavior.

Administrative Recruitment

What are the processes involved? Within a university setting there are many more problems to investigate than there are persons to engage in their study. The basic university structure which prepares the faculty and its members for administrative work and the structure which prepares the administration for a particular faculty member is the committee. To be sure there are many committees whose function it may be to criticize university policy. Nevertheless, the committee becomes the socializing agency which enables the administration to make its point of view known; and where the interested person may soon learn what is expected. There are at least two types of faculty members caught in the role conflict we have described whose behavior is oriented toward involvement in an administrative role.

The Comittee Man

One type of faculty member who may aspire to the administrative role is the general committee man. Such a faculty member *seeks committee membership;* he enjoys the prestige associated with committee assignments. He is quick to learn the wishes of those above him and he behaves accordingly. He enjoys the preparation of reports and dialogue with the administration. He employs objectivity in the service of seeming rational and neutral. The hope is that his seemingly exemplary behavior will offend no one and that the administration will be impressed.

The General Volunteer

A second type of faculty member who aspires to the administrative role is the general volunteer. The volunteer is most readily identified by his fervent desire to help the university improve itself. He is usually in possession of a fund of information and ideas regarding funds for research, for buildings, for faculty. He is readily available, although he appears reluctant, to undertake surveys and investigations to assist the university.

Behavioral Requirements

The essential talent for those who seek the administrative role lies in making themselves available with services and information without constituting a threat to those above and without the display of open aggression toward the current administrative arrangement. The inability to deal with these problems creates an additional source of frustration for the administrative aspirants. For the inability to control their hostility and ambition results in losing favor. To move too fast, to criticize too readily may become sufficiently threatening and result in being dropped from serious consideration for administrative posts. Aspirants who meet with such disappointments will often reject the administrative role, turn against the administration, and assume the *role of spokesman* for the faculty. The new role may then be imbued with much significance. For example, the administration may then be viewed as unusually oppressive and not really interested in student or the faculty. Feeling left out, these individuals can readily take up causes and interestingly enough may do a great deal more good as faculty spokesmen by providing a constructive opposition than they might have as administrators. *Thus, it might well be that inside every faculty spokesman frustrated administrative ambitions are present.*

Although the administrative role and the faculty spokesman role appear to have little in common each may achieve similar results for the individual who seeks prestige, without enduring the hazards of research and writing. Either role helps remove the individual from the responsibility of further research and writing. Although this may be simpler for the administrator, it is still quite possible for the faculty spokesman. He becomes heavily implicated in meetings and organizing campaigns on numerous issues, university reorganization, student faculty relations, faculty salaries, and so forth. Nevertheless, in so doing what frequently starts out being simply a drive for power and prestige becomes manifest in socially constructive patterns in which real benefits accrue not only to the individual faculty member but to the general faculty as well.

22

Summary and Conclusion

We have tried to outline the plight of the academic man in America by examining the move for status and prestige in a dual value system *which praises* the role of teacher *but rewards* the faculty member for research and writing. We have tried to point out the implications of such duality for both the university and the faculty; and we have also tried to examine the adaptations which are made by both the faculty and administration.

In an expanding situation, with increasing enrollments and university growth, *adaptations to such plights and conflicts may be* more readily conceived. Many faculty can move into administrative structures or remain in their teaching roles albeit that the latter may have fewer rewards. Given a decline in enrollments and a constriction of growth universities may once more revert to criteria of research and writing for promotion and rewards. Under such conditions administrative and teaching roles may be too few to absorb aspirants. Moreover, even these roles may be allocated to those who already have established themselves in research and writing.

Finally, it should be noted that the conflict in which the academic man in America finds himself is also at the heart of some of the problems of the modern university. Some amount of faulty and meaningless research is inevitable under any system, the same argument can be made for teaching. But when the choice of one (research and writing) or the other is overly determined either by a compulsive need for prestige and status and the other (teaching) by default, then the entire university system may become subverted to ends for which it was never intended. The responsibility for this state of affairs represents a most serious social problem for which the entire university community bears some responsibility.

CHAPTER 4

Ideological Factors of the Administration and Faculty

In viewing the total academic setting one often assumes more integration than may in fact be present. Certainly with respect to the administration and faculty there may be sharp differences of opinion; and these may vary from one institutional setting to another. It is important to examine these differences since they enable us to understand some of the problems that emerge between the administration and its faculty.

University administrative systems are concerned with at least the following: managements and coordination of university functions, and the implementation of educational philosophy and change. The extent to which an administration initiates innovation in educational philosophy is problematic since it may be lacking in knowledge, limited in interest, or hampered by greater ongoing institutional demands which require a high priority. At the present time, with considerable campus unrest, more administrations have been sensitized to the need for reevaluation of their programs, but their responses may be reactive rather than innovative. We recognize, of course, that some university administrations, more than others, are quite innovative.

Management Functions

Management functions in the university administration are manifest in the preoccupation with fiscal matters, salaries, raises, promotions, teaching loads, allocation of staff, and the like. These concerns may frequently lead contemporary administrators to become preoccupied with basically *non-academic and non-intellectual pursuits.* Significant though these preoccupations be for operating the institution, they result in a concern for efficiency.

The managerial ideology becomes a frame of reference toward which the administrator gravitates. Such preoccupations effect all levels of administration but are probably concentrated most heavily among the chairmen, deans, and vice-presidents, although not all administrators respond in identical ways to be sure.

The managerial ideology of the university administration leads to a series of difficulties.

(1) One such difficulty is that administrators often remove themselves from the basic concerns of the academic-scholarly community and its faculty. To be sure in a general way administrators share concerns with the faculty, but often these are the concerns of an entrepreneur who has a group of employees. Each is concerned for salaries and related conditions, but each has a different perspective. The administration is concerned with management and coordination, the scholarly-academic community is concerned with conditions surrounding the creation and transmission of knowledge and commensurate rewards.

(2) A second difficulty is that the concern for efficiency among the administration results in patterns to minimize input while maximizing output. Thus, the conditions of the market enter. Salaries become a function of the number of faculty available at given levels of skill and productivity.

The marketing orientation of the administration is manifest in the way it deals with the faculty on these matters. Since faculty demands on the administration for salary increases and promotions are persistent, and since the administration has realistic constraints upon the rewards it may distribute, decisions with regard to their distribution have to be made. A basic administrative requirement is that faculty demands be managed so that they do not get out of hand. It is partly for this reason that a compliant chairman is generally more acceptable to the higher administration than an aggressive chairman who makes demands for members of his department. It is perhaps when a department begins to stagnate in an institution with otherwise good departments that a search for an aggressive chairman probably will be undertaken. Even here aggressivity will be tolerated within limits.

A compliant chairman becomes functional within the university structure because he makes few demands on the administration. Further, although it may appear paradoxical, an administration can be especially alert to detect faculty members who are in some sense not doing all they might be. Thus, an unfavorable teaching report on a faculty member may be welcomed, misbehavior may be welcomed, incompetence may even be welcomed, not because a particular administrator has a need to punish a faculty member, rather it is because the administrative system invariably has a greater number clamoring for rewards than there are rewards to distribute; and each faculty member who engages in behavior that is unacceptable permits the administrator to remove rewards, rewards that may now be used elsewhere. The administrator who has four promotions to distribute and fifteen people who have been recommended may unconsciously welcome the knowledge that at least two recommended faculty have been reported for poor teaching.

I am not saying that administrators are not concerned with incompetence per se, they are, but at least some incompetence is functional. A university of all competent faculty would create very serious problems for an administration.

Less competent faculty can also at times be used by a higher administration to temper rewards for stronger faculty members. Thus, an administrator can justify the reduction of a recommendation for a high raise on the part of a productive faculty member by pointing to needs of other less competent faculty members for cost of living increases. If necessary the administration can devise its own rules for coping with what it deems excessive faculty demands. Administrators can, for example, control promotions or raises by simply saying that a particular faculty member has moved too rapidly in relation to other faculty members.

(3) The managerial ideology with a preoccupation for efficiency may result in caricatures of the faculty by the administration without their being fully aware of the implications. Faculty members may easily be viewed essentially in laymen's terms; as impractical, inefficient, as men who are valuable in their own way, but who are removed from real concerns. The view may become quite anti-intellectual, and in many instances not totally different from the reactionary segments of the academic community.

(4) The managerial ideology carries with it a concern for order, regulation, and control that is the essence of management. This in part helps explain a university's interest in an endless variety of applied programs; speech and hearing difficulties, personal counseling, programs for delinquency, crime and corrections; while often neglecting other parts of university growth. More recently the existence of massive public grants for poverty and the problems of the cities has made a good fit with the managerial ideology and the older tradition of pragmatism in American education. Each has complimented the other. Whatever altruism and

good will there may be, the preoccupation with correcting the faults of society, of improving society, stem from a university's basic belief in management and control, quite apart from the funding benefits that may accrue. It may also make a university administration very sympathetic with those members of the faculty who want to engage in work of an applied nature. I am not passing judgment on the university's involvement in applied programs. These would have to be evaluated on their individual merits. I am simply commenting on why the involvement is a good fit for the administration.

(5) A fifth difficulty associated with the managerial ideology has to do with role conflict for the administrator. The conflict may be one between the values of the managerial ideology concerned with coordination and efficiency and scholarly-academic values in which efficiency does not achieve the highest priority. For the administrator there is probably an ongoing ambivalence, perhaps in part a function of having been socialized in two different traditions, the managerial and the scholarly-academic; perhaps the ambivalence stems from the guilt of having abandoned an academic career in search of other values; perhaps it is a combination of several of these points.

Much of the ambivalence which administrators have about their own roles is the product of a system they have helped create, and which they tend to support in their efforts to raise the stature of their own units and universities. Thus, they are heavily implicated in the creation of an atmosphere that places a high priority on research and writing; an activity in which they fail to partake by and large. The result may often be a negative image of self and role.

The extent to which such ambivalence is present is manifest in a variety of ways, and makes the administrator unnecessarily defensive in dealing with the faculty; since often he may have very real doubts about his contributions to the university. The administrator's business and managerial talents are an indispensible ingredient of the successful university; but as the administrative components and the scholarly-academic components have become separated, the split has become more pronounced. This separation is in part at the heart of some of the contemporary problems on American campuses. Many students and faculty have serious doubts about the moral, and even legal, authority of the administration in contemporary university affairs.

Although we have focused on administrative difficulties stemming from their managerial orientation, significant contributions are made; both the faculty and the administration may not fully appreciate the contribution. For example, the management functions are clearly necessary and contribute significantly to the ongoing operation of the university. Funding is essential in attracting and holding competent faculty. Protection from the attacks of reactionary elements represents an ongoing battle. These are vital functions. In addition, many institutions left to the wishes of the faculty would remain unchanged; this is particularly the case at smaller institutions that have been stagnant for many years. Often there is inertia, and it is often an enlightened administration which drags a faculty kicking and screaming into new and significant fields of enterprise.

The Faculty

Thus far we have addressed ourselves to the university administrator and the system in which he operates. The faculty has its own system predicated on assumptions that are similar to the higher administrations', but also different.

A good many faculty share the managerial ideology of the higher administration in that they see the goal of the university as centering less around the creation of basic knowledge and more on values of the managerial ideology. These faculty see the university as ever assisting with the amelioration of social problems, of helping society to function more smoothly. Thus, they participate in precisely those research and demonstration projects consistent with such an ideology. Their many university and community involvements may also reflect such an orientation.

There is a second category of faculty who see the university less in a managerial or scholarly-academic sense and more in terms of essentially a setting for instruction.

A third group see the university in more traditional terms of a complex in which knowledge and ideas are created and disseminated; that is, they place emphasis on teaching-research, with heavy emphasis on research.

The faculty of American universities are heterogeneous. There may be sharp disagreements and differences of opinion between the faculty on the functions of the university.

While each category of faculty may differ with respect to ideology, each shares some things in common with regard to their view of the administration. Just as the administration has to be seen as holding power and controlling rewards, so the faculty have to be viewed in terms of challenges to power. Such challenges almost never take the form of overt struggles; by and large faculty members have avoided unions. Instead faculty groups behave in different ways; and each of the three faculty groups we have identified responds differently to their frustrated ambitions for power, prestige, and status. Each also has its reaction to the power of the administration. Those with the managerial ideology may, of course, become administrators. The shift in orientation for them from faculty to administration would not be great.

Moreover, for many faculty who are already committed to a managerial orientation, the shift into administration does not basically suggest a drastic change in career. It is simply a shift to an administrative level of operations.

The question of why many faculty have accepted a managerial ideology may be related to broader social trends, where rewards for managerial talent can be extremely high. Certainly the pragmatism which has been pronounced in American society for a long time is important. Education is viewed as a panacea for all social ills; and education means the application of knowledge. These are things to which Americans are attuned and understand.

In addition only small sections of any society are capable of creative and innovative work in the basic sciences. In spite of relatively large numbers of faculty today, the percentage of those capable of meeting the research demands has probably not changed. Thus, there are many faculty who find a calling in other aspects of university life. While many administrative posts call for the highest talent, many can be filled with less; and a significant number may require very little. The continuing demands for excellence which the academic professions expect cause the high number of faculty who cannot meet these demands, to find the ever available openings in administration unusual opportunities, as indicated in an earlier section of this book.

Those with a managerial ideology not interested in administration may maximize their worth to their university and increase their power and prestige by bringing in large grants for demonstration projects in social problems areas; endeavors consistent with the management and control of society. By attracting large grants these people become important to the university while supporting the managerial ideology. By the same token the withdrawal of these people from the university may mean a significant loss to the institution. The faculty member responds to the marketing situation by making himself more marketable; and such marketability means that demands for greater rewards, power and financial, can be made.

Similarly those faculty involved basically in research and writing respond by increasing their marketability through publications, grants, and by occupying significant positions in major professional organizations on a national and international level. They, even more than most, are in a position to press the university for rewards since their departure can be more devastating.

Those primarily involved in teaching have relatively little power in relation to the two categories we have been describing. While their departure from the university may involve some loss, it is usually a loss that is easily replaced. It is only during periods of extreme faculty shortage that the departure of those who are primarily teachers becomes serious. I am not in any sense trying to assess the ultimate contribution of the teacher in comparison to other faculty engaged in different activities. My comments refer only to the position in which those involved essentially in teaching find themselves. Since the power of such faculty is limited, they may welcome student assertions that good teaching is being abandoned, that the university in quest of growth has become too large and too impersonal. The views themselves have considerable validity but they may have special meaning for faculty without power. Probably such views do little to increase the power of these faculty, but the views may make their existence a bit more pleasant.

I have indicated that in many ways the faculty are concerned for power. Thus, it would be expected that the faculty would hold certain views of the administration. The faculty are first fearful of the administration. Fear stems from the concern that power may be used against them. There is also hostility based on the fact that often the faculty member may be impotent to respond to administrative power employed against him. In the vast majority of ongoing decisions that are made by the administration the faculty members ability to respond is limited. Yet the attitude toward the administration is also an ambivalent one. The faculty may have admiration for administration; admiration for the administrators' capacity to achieve power and to employ it.

Finally, it is of interest to note that in the eyes of the faculty, the administration has great power but little prestige. From the vantage point of the administrator tha faculty member has little power but considerable prestige. Insofar as these views continue to be held, it becomes difficult for individuals in either of these roles (administrator or scholar) to be wholly comfortable in their respective roles.

Finally, we might add that each group, administration and faculty, operates with its own set of premises, rules, and patterns. Each is in some basic sense interested in the educational process, in the university, and in the student; but neither group is exclusively concerned with these matters; and there remains the ongoing necessity to afford personal concerns a realistic place in the goals and aims of the total university complex.

This brings to close the first section of this book which attempts to deal with the university setting in America, along with the efforts made by the administration and faculty to deal with the problems that beset them.

The remaining sections of this book are devoted to Professor Gunnar Boalt's reports drawn from Swedish society.

References

Babchuck, Nicholas, and Alan Bates. 1962. Professor or producer. The two faces of academic man. *Social Forces,* Vol. 40 (May), p. 341–348.

Berelson, Bernard. 1960. *Graduate Education in the United States.* New York: McGraw-Hill.

Bernard, Jesse. 1964. *Academic Women,* The Pennsylvania State University Press.

Boalt, Gunnar. 1965. The sociology of research. *Acta Sociologica,* Vol. 8, No. 2, p. 257–284.

— 1969. *The Sociology of Research.* Carbondale: Southern Illinois University Press.

Brown, David G. 1965. *Academic Labor Markets,* A report to the office of manpower automation and training, U.S. Department of Labor.

— 1967. *The Mobile Professors.* Washinton, D.C.: American Council on Education.

Caplow, Theodore, and Reese J. McGee. 1958. *The Academic Market Place.* New York: Basic Books.

Corson, J. G. 1960. *Governance of Colleges and Universitites.* MacGraw-Hill.

Dibden, Arthur J. (editor). 1968. *The Academic Deanship in American Colleges and Universities.* Carbondale: Southern Illinois University Press.

Frankel, Charles. 1968. *Education and the Barricades.* W. W. Norton.

Goode, William. A theory of role strain. *American Sociological Review,* Vol. 25, No. 4, p. 483–496.

Gross, Edward. 1968. Universities as organizations: A research approach. *American Sociological Review,* Vol. 33, No. 4 (August), p. 518–544.

Gross, Edward, and Paul Giomsbach. *Academic Administrator and University Goals.* Washington, D.C.: American Council on Education.

Hollingshead, A. B. 1938. In group membership and academic selection. *American Sociological Review,* Vol. 3.

Lazarsfeld, Paul F., and Wagner Thielens, Jr. 1958. *The Academic Mind.* Glencoe, Illinois: The Free Press.

Record, Wilson. 1960. Some reflections of bureaucratic trends in sociological research. *American Sociological Review,* Vol. 25, No. 3 (June).

— 1963. Foundation support of social science research in the U.S.A.: A critique. *Sociologia Internationales,* Vol. 1, No. 1 (Summer).

Reder, Melvin W. 1955. *The theory of occupational wage differentials. American Economic Review,* Vol. XLV, December.

Segerstedt, Torgny T. 1966. *Den akademiska gemenskapen.* Uppsala universitets Årsböcker Uppsala.

Sugarman, Barry N. 1962. *Goal Conflict in Complex Organizations: A Case Study of an American State University* (unpublished M. A. thesis). Department of Sociology, Southern Illinois University.

The Wall Street Journal. 1965. June, 3. (This discussion deals with the changing role of the professor in society.)

Wilson, Logan. 1942. *The Academic Man: A Study in the Sociology of a Profession.* New York: Oxford University Press.

— 1961. *Academic Man Revisited.* Paper presented at the Institute for College and University Administrators at University of California, Berkeley, California. (July 31–Aug. 4.)

CHAPTER 5

Can We Study the Adaptation Process?

In the previous chapters we noted that academic people had several important roles to perform: researcher, teacher, administrator, faculty spokesman, a good fellow, or combinations of these. Some faculty are able to perform some of these roles well, engaging in research and lending a hand to the chairman on an administrative problem. But only some of these roles do bring rewards. If he is not able to publish, he will in the long run give up research; if he does not feel, or believe, that the students receive something from his courses, he may become cynical about teaching. If his ideas are not popular in the faculty, he will be silent there; and if his good companionship is not appreciated he will probably transfer it to some more positive milieu. He simply tries to use his personal resources so that they bring him rewards. Research rewards have the highest regard, then probably administrative rewards such as the office of chairman, of dean, etc. Rewards for being a good teacher certainly are rare and/or difficult to measure. The faculty spokesman gets his rewards when his ideas are taken seriously. The good companion, of course, is not taken very seriously and there are few rewards coming to a man who has neither research, teaching, nor administrative merits, but only a pleasing manner and a wish to suit everybody.

If research rewards are significant, many younger faculty try to engage in research although only a few succeed. Failure in the research role brings with it a shift into other roles. In this manuscript we have stressed the shift away from research to administration; and we have suggested that such a shift is not reversible in any simple way. The administrator may lose touch with the field; and it becomes increasingly difficult for him to move back into such activities. Thus, he remains in administration. If he can't, and if he is fortunate, he may become a wise and respected member of the faculty. In the same way the researcher does not take refuge in teaching unless he has to give up research; and after some years of teaching, his chances for research have diminished further.

Can the shifts in role behavior we have been describing be measured?

Scales for Measuring Faculty Behavior

We need scales for measuring two aspects of the faculty members' behaviors:

(1) The amount of energy or resources he uses for research, administration, teaching, spokesmanship, or companionship.

(2) The output or reward he gets from his effort in each of these fields.

The first set of scales must be based either on observation or on questionnaire data.

The second set of scales could use publications, grants, or honorary scientific posts as measures of research rewards. Administrative promotion, administrative committee memberships, and the like might reflect the administrative rewards. But how can we measure teaching rewards? Large classes are not reported anywhere but carefully filed away. The preparation of textbooks seems to be the only kind of teaching reward that can be shown by the efficient teacher—and only few are given the chance for that kind of merit. Besides, textbooks not only have to be good but they should sell also; and they are easier to sell if the author, or authors, have established reputations. Thus, there may be a positive correlation between research rewards and teaching rewards if these are measured with textbook production.

The role of faculty spokesman could probably be measured in the number of short, sharp articles in newspapers, university dailes, etc., calling attention to this or that bad practice, pointing out the hidden meaning behind the official smoke screen, etc. But articles of this kind are epheremal, seldom mentioned and difficult to register. We are afraid a scale like that would be of little help. The reward or the output for the role of good companion is still more difficult to measure—as there seems to be no reward at all; and it is very difficult to register the output of well meant routine kindness. So we have to abandon the measurement of this last role. Perhaps the role of good companion does not even exist in the sense that there may be no reward for friendly behavior in the faculty if you are neither researcher, administrator, teacher, nor a faculty spokesman.

The Interaction Between Role Behaviors

Let us presume that we have a sample of sociology departments, that we have scales for measuring, or at least estimating, the behaviors of the faculty members during the last five years, like research publication, grants, honorary scientific posts, administrative promotion, committeeship, teaching, newspaper articles—and leaving the university for a position outside the academic world.

We expect then that the first three behaviors (publication, grants, and honorary scientific posts) will tend to correlate with each other. But they should show negative correlations with administrative promotion, with committeeships, with the preparation of newspaper articles, and with the transfer to a non-academic job. All of these latter variables, (4, 5, 6, 7 and 8 in Table 1), however intrinsically significant, tend to decrease ones capacity to function effectively in the roles associated with the first three variables.

We can thus construct a simple matrix for these eight variables with their 8×8 correlations and mark the sign, positive or negative, that we

Table 1. *Matrix for expected signs of correlations between faculty behaviors belonging to five different clusters*

No.	Variable	1 Publi- cation	2 Grants	3 Hon- orary posts	4 Promo- tion	5 Com- mittee	6 Teacher only	7 Dailies	8 Leav- ing
1	Research publications	/////	+	+	–	–	–	–	–
2	Received grants	+	/////	+	–	–	–	–	–
3	Honorary professional posts	+	+	/////	–	–	–	–	–
4	Promotion to administra- tion	–	–	–	/////	+	–	–	–
5	Committee assignments	–	–	–	+	/////	–	–	–
6	Teacher only	–	–	–	–	–	/////	–	–
7	Preparation of newspaper articles	–	–	–	–	–	–	/////	–
8	Leaving academic work	–	–	–	–	–	–	–	/////

35

might expect between them. We may keep the variables together in five clusters as they are meant to measure the role of research (1 publications, 2 grants, and 3 scientific honorary posts), of administration (4 promotions, 5 committeeships), of teaching, of spokesmanship (7 dailies), and of outsider (8 leaving for another job). The matrix of our expected correlations can be seen in Table 1.

This matrix then demonstrates the possible positive correlations between the variables belonging to the *same* cluster and the negative correlations between variables belonging to *different* clusters. The matrix could afford considerable information about the interaction between variables. Moreover, it gives us insight in how one behavior—or a cluster of allied behaviors—might compensate for lack of another one.

If we *did* find clearcut clusters with negative correlations between variables from different clusters (suggesting that the clusters are to some extent able to compensate lack of each other), how could we measure the variables' compensation power?

Compensation Power of Behavior Variables

There seems to be at least two different ways of computing the importance of a behavior. We can either try to make an overall estimation of what general status each member has in the faculty and then see how strong a correlation each behavior variable has with this criterion; or we might try to use the matrix itself for the procedure.

The first method assumes that the type of behaviors we study here are used by the faculty members in order to get rewards; and that these rewards ought to show in the status each member enjoys in his faculty. The status thus should be a kind of sum made up by the output on the rewards of those behaviors we have listed. If a behavior gives a lot of status, it should accordingly show strong positive correlation with this estimated general status, but if it has little effect on the status—and the behavior is found among those that have few other sources of status—then the correlation should be negative. A zero correlation would *not* mean that the behavior did not give status, only that the status it gave was barely enough to compensate for lack of other status sources. If we were able to compute for the behavior variables this way their correlations with some general criterion, as just indicated, it might be possible to place them in rank order from the high esteemed variables, correlated strongly with status, down to the low esteemed, correlated negatively.

This technique of computing the importance of a variable in interaction with other variables may be called *criterion importance*.

The second method of measuring the importance of a behavior and its status would be to try to extract some kind of measure out of the matrix. We could reason this way: if a behavior is important for status in the faculty, then the member who has it can afford to give up other ways of status seeking and the member who does not have it must try to compensate with strong efforts along other lines. Such reasoning would not apply to more insecure faculty members. Thus, the more important a behavior is, the stronger negative correlations it ought to show with the variables belonging to other clusters. Of course, a variable sometimes might have many, or even mostly, positive correlations with the variables belonging to other clusters, showing that it belongs to them too, and thus has little importance for compensating them. We should then be able to use the mean of the correlations between one variable and all the variables in other clusters—with the sign changed—as an indication of this variable's compensation power in the interaction with other variables. We could then put the variables in rank order, starting with important behavior variables negatively correlated with the variables in other clusters, and ending with unimportant variables even positively correlated. This method of computing importance we may call *interaction weight*.

But, suppose we did both computations, would not criterion importance and interaction weight give the same rank order? In theory, yes, but only if both of the two methods could be used properly. The risks may be noted here:

(1) If the criterion does not measure what it should, the rank order will be confused. We may try to estimate the status of faculty members not according to their role behavior as researchers, administrators, teachers, spokesmen, etc., but we may use instead the classification: chairman, full professor, associate professor, assistant professor, and at the bottom, instructor. Should we do this, the picture of status changes. The beautiful pattern of compensating clusters might dissolve and if there still survived some resemblance of them, the rank order of their variables would certainly change. Thus, the results that are obtained are in part a function of the classification of role behaviors employed.

(2) When we compute interaction weights out of the matrix, we assume that all faculty members give the same weight to each variable. But is this really realistic? Take the role of faculty spokesman. He certainly may have a high regard for himself in terms of this role, but do the

others? Up to a point each faculty member should overrate the role or roles he does perform, and underrate those he does not. And this is an important part of the adaptation process. The tendency to evaluate roles differently makes it necessary to apply our method of measuring interaction weights only on those variables that are valued about the same way by the whole sample. There must be a consensus, otherwise the rank order may become meaningless.

The Summation Theory

Actually this discussion has introduced a new note that we call "summation" theory; if we want to study interaction of variables, we should try to study them all at the same time. This theory has been advocated earlier in Gunnar Boalt, *Family and Marriage,* New York: McKay, 1965, Chs. 3 and 4; also in Gunnar Boalt, *Sociology of Research,* Carbondale, Ill.: Southern Illinois University Press, 1969. We introduce it in the following chapters.

CHAPTER 6

The Researcher's Role

as Reflected in the Production of M.A. and Ph.D. Theses

How does the researcher proceed? Few sociologists have been interested in that problem although every elementary textbook is full of advice regarding what the researcher *should* do: bring a theory out of his hat, formulate his hypotheses in advance, test reliability and validity of his instruments, draw a representative sample, find something useful for his society and report his findings so that other researchers can replicate his investigation.

All this well meant and sometimes useful advice can be taken either as rules for the researcher's behavior or as values, scientific values, that he tries to reach. Let us handle them as values then, such as hypotheses formulated in advance, reliability, validity, correct sample, use for society, etc. In theory every scientific project then should cover every scientific value. Well, researchers know they don't. At the planning stage each scientific value makes demands on the meager resources of the project and thus has to be balanced carefully against other values. You do not have enough time to cover the theoretical field and the empirical field at the same time. If you have hit upon a brand new idea, you are so very anxious to get going before anyone else stumbles upon it that you willingly sacrifice a lot of reliability and validity in order to get the report printed as soon as possible. Thus, one value often is able to replace or compensate for another and so we are back to the summation theory again.

But beware, there is a difficulty here that must be pointed out before we start discussing scientific values in detail: the effect of the sampling upon the interaction of the value grades.

If we take a sample of all kinds of sociological research, from small papers in college journals, to M.A. theses, articles, and large sized reports, these projects evidently cover the whole scale for available re-sources: the top projects had large amounts of money, the bottom pro-jects little or none. Then the projects with large economic resources probably will be able to score high grades on many scientific values; the projects with medium resources will tend to score in the middle; and the projects with none or little money will tend to score low. And so all scientific values will tend to follow each other, simply because the top group has so high scores and the bottom group so few. For a sample of projects where all resource levels are represented we should expect only positive correlations between the scores of all the scientific values, that is, they should form just one single cluster.

But we still believe that actually the values often tend to counteract or compensate each other. Only that cannot be shown in a sample where projects on all resource levels are included. We have instead to select our sample from *one* stratum, not from all of them, for instance take one sample of Ph.D. theses, another of M.A. theses, a third from top journals etc., and then study each sample *per se.*

Let us stick to the sample of Ph.D. theses. Of course, they do vary in resources, if you just mean the actual costs. But if you look at time spent, energy used, etc., the differences might be smaller. And then the Ph.D. candidate would have to allocate these resources of his as care-fully as possible to cope with the scientific values so that those given more emphasis by his training, his committee or his problem have a proper chance to get a high score. That would bring forth negative correlations between competing or compensating clusters of values, show-ing a beautiful pattern in the matrix.

If we select a sample of projects somewhere in the middle between these two extremes, we probably would find the clusters from the stratum sample still showing but the negative correlations between variables from different clusters on the way to turn positive or already past that point.

From the statistician's point of view we evidently expect correlations between variables from different clusters to be *negative within resource classes,* but *positive between resource classes.*

Scientific values in a sample of Swedish sociological Ph.D. theses

Grants from the Central Union of Social Work and from the Bank of Sweden Tercentenary Fund made it possible to take a sample consisting of the 21 Swedish sociological Ph.D. theses that had appeared up to

40

1966, work out preliminary scales of values, test their reliability and modify the scales if it seemed necessary. We used 29 scales and to these we added 3 other scales (year, mark, grade sum), making 32.

We divided the values according to the discussion previously given (in G. Boalt: *Sociology of Research.* Carbondale, Illinois: The Southern Illinois University Press, 1969), in three groups: *Planning values, work values,* and *additional values.*

Planning Values

Planning values are those values that are taken into account already during the planning stage. We have devised scales for measuring 13 planning values, but have placed these scales in an appendix. Here we just mention each value, hint at how it is measured and give the reliability found as product moment coefficient when Dr. Robert Erikson and I independently of each other used the scales on the 21 theses.

(1) *Presentation of the hypotheses.* Five steps from low grade (or the project does not intend to test hypotheses) to high with 5 theses at the lowest grade, then 3, 9, 0 and 4. Reliability + .88.

(2) *Reliability.* Five steps from low to high with 1, 3, 10, 1 and 6 theses at the five grades. Reliability of the reliability scale + .56.

(3) *Validity of dependent and independent variables.* One or several of them. Five steps from low to high with 9, 0, 7, 1, 4 theses at the five grades. Reliability + .74.

(4) *Sampling procedure.* Three steps from bad to good, 8 theses in the lowest grade, 4 in the middle, and 9 in the top. Reliability + .72.

(5) *Generalization of the situation.* Three steps from no discussion of the problem to lengthy discussion. With 9 theses at the lowest grade, 2 at the middle, and 10 at the highest grade. Reliability + .73.

(6) *Integration of the problem with a theory.* Five steps from an isolated problem not connected with a theory to a problem consisting only in testing a theory. The lowest grade had 8 theses, then came 4, 2, 5, and 2 for the following grades. Reliability + .57.

(7) *Investigation's value for theory construction in general.* Three steps from value neither implied nor asserted to value asserted. 20 theses got grade 1, the remaining single one got grade 3. Reliability + 1.00.

(8) *Investigation's value for hypothesis formation in general.* Three steps from value neither implied nor asserted. Twenty theses got grade 1, the remaining one the middle grade. Reliability + .98.

(9) *Investigation's value for statistical model formation in general.* Three

41

steps from value neither implied nor asserted. Twenty theses had grade 1, the remaining one the middle degree. Reliability + .98.

(10) *Investigation's value for variable construction in general.* Three steps from value neither implied nor asserted. Twenty theses got the lowest grade. The remaining one the highest. Reliability + 1.00.

(11) *Investigation's usefulness to society.* Five steps from social use neither suggested nor implied to social use supported either by numerical calculations or implied through official assignments. The theses came in with 6 at the lowest grade, then 5, 4, 5 and 1. Reliability + .67.

(12) *Problem's news value.* Five steps from problem same as before, tested with same methods, to problem new, largely new methods. The lowest grade had 3 theses, the following steps 13, 5, 0, 0. Reliability only .29. Scale revised after that, but not possible to get independent estimations of this new and presumably better scale.

(13) *Research orientation's utility.* Five steps ranging from the orientation of no special concern to the chairman's framework (a European phenomenon), to one in which the research orientation has to be defended on a broad front. This value alien to American sociologists, but certainly not to Swedish, although 13 theses got the lowest grade, then came 2, 1, 5, and 0. Reliability + .82.

Altogether the mean of these 13 reliability coefficients was + .76, which can be accepted.

These 13 values are so important that the researcher has to decide in his plan for the investigation which grade of each value he is aiming for. If he needs a grant for the project, he has to produce his plan and state his aspired values and grades. But of course his aspiration level is one thing, his achievement level another. He does not receive what he had expected from some of his values. The reliability turns out lower than he had expected; the sampling procedure does not work as it should, etc. Thus we will generally be able to measure the planning values twice, first the aspired grades at the planning stage, then the grades really achieved. The researcher seldom is able to achieve more than he expected and generally far less of some or many values. What does he do then? Well, actually his reactions will affect not only the planning values but *all* his scientific values.

Working Values

Researchers of course often plan their data handling techniques in advance but generally do not commit themselves in the project plan they hand in, when asking for a grant. Thus, working techniques generally can be asserted only in the account of the investigation given in the final report. We used for our set of Swedish projects the following ten working values.

(14) *Definitions of the variables.* Five steps from no operational definitions to all variables defined both operationally and nominally. Two of the theses had the lowest grade, then came 2, 6, 5, and 6 in the remaining four. Reliability .76.

(15) *Mathematical models.* Six steps from no discussion of a mathematical model up to the complicated level of integral. Fourteen of the theses stayed at grade 1, then 4, 0, 0, 2 and 1. Reliability .96.

(16) *Statistical model.* Four steps from no statistical model, a model neither deterministic nor probabilistic, a deterministic one and—at the top—a probabilistic one. 18 of our theses at grade 1, none at grade 2, two had a deterministic model and one a probabilistic. Reliability .52.

(17) *Scaling technique for treating data.* Five steps from no scales to ratio scales for some main variables. Three theses at grade 1, then 10, 8, 0, 0. Reliability .53.

(18) *Analysis method's value.* Five steps from incorrect methods to a method not only well adapted to the problem but also new in important respects. Five theses got grade 1; the following grades attained by 5, 9, 2, and 0. Reliability .66.

(19) *Mathematical treatment of data.* Six steps according to the difficulty of the operations from no mathematical treatment to matrix calculus. Our 21 theses were distributed with 3, 2, 14, 1, 1, and 0 on these grades. Reliability .69.

(20) *Material's size.* Five steps from less than 51 observations to more than 1000. The lowest grade was given 1 thesis, then came 1, 2, 7, and 10. Reliability .87.

(21) *Non-response in the material.* Six steps from non-response not reported to a drop-out of less than 2 %. Our theses had two cases of grade 1, then came 2, 6, 6, 2, and 3. Reliability .54.

(22) *Fate of the hypotheses.* Sociology text books certainly tell us that the researcher thinks it just as rewarding to have his hypotheses rejected as to get them accepted when he tests them. However, we do not believe this and construct our own scale for this important value from the bottom where half or more of the hypotheses are rejected to the paradise where nearly all hypotheses are accepted at a significance level of $p < 0.01$.

No less than twelve of our 21 theses belonged to grade 1, then came 5, 2, 1, and 1. Reliability .50.

The mean reliability coefficient of these ten scales for working values is .69. But probably a little more as we have revised them using the cases, where Robert Erikson and Gunnar Boalt disagreed, to point out weaknesses and get rid of them.

Additional values

Those scientific values that can be brought into action during the last stage of the investigation: the hammering out and brush up of the report. We have tried the following six additional values:

(23) *Information additional to planned report.* Five steps from no information added to new variables introduced. The text books advise us that a good project should hold to its original problem and not tackle new problems, but theses authors seem to think otherwise and we heed them—although they are wrong. Actually sixteen of the theses gave no additional information, but in the following grades we got 3, 1, 1, and 0. Reliability originally only .04. We revised the scale on several points and gave it the form reported in the appendix, but had discussed the material so thoroughly that it was of little use to estimate the grades "independently".

(24) *Citation of literature.* We classify this value according to the number of references at the end of the publication, or given in the text. Eight steps from no references given to more than 200. The first four grades contained none of our theses and the eight grades thus came out: 0, 0, 0, 0, 3, 7, 9, 2. Reliability .89.

(25) *Value of language.* (From the Swedish point of view.) He who publishes in Swedish shows that he does not believe his work to be of any interest outside Sweden. We thus place this at the bottom. A summary in any foreign language gives grade 2 and at the top, grade 6, we find works published in English, German, or French with technical terms well translated and in a good style. Two theses came in grade 1, then came 10, 0, 0, 5, and 4. Reliability .98.

(26) *Number of pages.* (Large pages multiplied by 2). Eight steps from 10 pages or less to more than 500 pages. Theses must have a certain size and so none of them came in the first three grades. The distribution was 0, 0, 0, 1, 2, 5, 12, 1. Reliability .99.

(27) *Value of researcher's title (degree)*. High degrees or titles should help to compensate weaknesses in reports—or at least we thought so. We used five steps, from authors being neither M.A. nor assistant teachers to full professors. But in this particular case the title is of little use for the scale as by definition all Ph.D. candidates are M.A. Thus we have no reliability data for this scale.

(28) *Ability of researcher to disguise deficiencies of the project*. The reader of the theses often saw little or nothing seriously wrong with the projects. We found it necessary then to introduce a "value", evidently important to the Ph.D. candidates; how well could they hide the deficiences of their investigations. We used five steps in our scale, going from no ability (which we consider a compliment to the author) to very high. Four theses got grade 1; the following grades got 7, 4, 4, and 2. Reliability .61.

We have been able to measure reliability only for five additional scientific values and they have a mean of .70. Probably reliability for the scale of value 24 now is higher than .04, which should raise the mean too.

Three remaining scales for year of publication, mark of thesis and sum of value grades

We end this enumeration by giving three more scales that might come in handy in our discussion:

(29) *Year of publication,* starting with the first thesis in 1947 and ending in the fifth grade, with the 21st in 1966.

(30) *Mark given the thesis by the faculty*. Swedish faculties use a scale of seven steps.

(31) *Sum of scientific value grades* on scales 1–29, listed above. Five steps.

The interaction between scientific values in a sample of Ph.D. theses

No researcher undertakes a project unless it seems to promise high grades from a number of important values, notably planning values. But, we seldom achieve all the grades we have aspired to, and so the value sum of the investigation quickly goes down once the project is started. Most of us have been more or less interested in several new projects before we made our definite choice and when this chosen alternative of ours meets reality, its realistic sum of value grades sinks below our aspired value sum of those projects that still have met no realistic testing.

It is a hard blow to see a beautiful project shrink down. The researcher tries to save his threatened grades. If for instance his variables turn out to be less reliable than he had expected, he tries to group them together in new combinations, etc. If the investigation takes a course making it less useful to society, he strives to find some other practical application of his project.

This experience brings with it a severe frustration to the scientist making his role of researcher painful, forcing him to exert all his resources to repair his threatened values. At these times he might feel himself incompetent and useless, he might project this on his teachers (who did not teach him enough science), his society (which does not really care about science) etc., he might pay less attention to his role of researcher and more to his other roles, etc. To employ the summation theory once more, we might say that researchers reassess their planning values as the research proceeds. Values that do not give the grade we hoped for are rationalized as not being very important. On the other hand, the values that do give us our expected grades are considered more important. We thus change the importance or the weight of the values according to the yield they gave us. Still, that will probably not compensate more than a part of our loss and so we look for other compensations. We have small chances to cram out more of the planning values, but the working values might come in handy and, of course, the additional values are always there—if you should need them badly.

To study this compensation process we should see how much each planning value is reduced in grade during the research process and then correlate all these changes (if any, nearly all to the worse) with the grades of working values and additional values that the researcher throws in, striving to keep up the total value grades of his project. We expect all these variables to interact, to show up in a matrix of the intercorrelations between all relevant variables. Value grades associated with each other for one reason or another should form clusters with positive correlations between each other, but variables belonging to different clusters would tend to have negative correlations, as they compete with each other for the project's resources or compensate for the lack of each other. Such a plan would have been ideal but not feasible.

We have instead been content with measuring all our available scientific values in the final report. We expect then that the final grades of the planning values will form one or more clusters in the matrix, with positive correlations within each cluster and negative correlations between variables from different clusters. Most working values and some additional ones will be more or less adopted into these clusters, but other additional values will be used to compensate for lacking grades in the large clusters and thus forced to form one or more clusters of their own, negatively correlated with the clusters of planning and working values. That is all that can be predicted out of our summation theory. But before we can have a look at the real matrix some points must be made:

(1) We have decided to place the variables in such an order that the possible clusters should show, in enumeration order within each cluster.
(2) We discussed at the end of the previous chapter how to measure the importance of each value and decided to try two: criterion importance and interaction weight. We intend here to use the mark given to the thesis by the faculty as a criterion of importance and intend to compute the interaction weight too, by taking the mean of the grades' correlations with values belonging to other clusters—sign changed from negative to positive or vice versa. This interaction weight is given in the last row of the matrix.
(3) All correlations are computed as tetrachoric coefficients, which means that all grade scales are dichotomized and that if one of the four resulting cells should happen to be empty, the correlation immediately goes to $+1.00$ or -1.00. The reader should keep this in mind and not be impressed by high correlations that can be obtained rather easily this way.

And then we should be prepared for a look at the matrix itself (Matrix 1).

The planning values are divided between three clusters, which have swallowed all working values and all additional values but two, 24 and 27, which can be said to form two small clusters of their own.

But are these five clusters, clusters in the sense we meant? Has it really been possible to select them so? Are all—or nearly all—correlations between the variables belonging to the *same* cluster *positive*? Are all—or nearly all—correlations between variables belonging to *different* clusters *negative*?

Well, the first cluster contains six planning values, most of the working values and one additional value, number of references. We could simply consider this as a cluster of the *empirical* scientific values that tend to follow each other because we are trained to respect them and try to do so in our resource allocation. The second cluster (4 sampling, 11 usefulness to society and 21 material's size) makes also sense because the sociologist who works for official agencies will not only look out for *social* use of his data but also has to convince the authorities that his results can be generalized and—as the authorities know nothing of sampling—must have a "strong" ground of many observations. The third cluster contains the four *theoretical* values 7–10, the planning value, 13, of taking care of the research school's interests and then the additional values 26 (language) and 29 (disguise of defects).

Before we make too much out of this set, let us point out that the four theoretical values 7–10 are represented by one single thesis and this cluster thus easily explained by coincidence. But let us for a while keep this theoretical cluster all the same in order to see if it does pop up in other samples too, which would force us to take it seriously, after all. The last two one-value clusters certainly make sense in Swedish Sociology: if the thesis did give too little information, try to squeeze some additional information out of it and if it is thin in all respects, write as many pages as possible! Well, the sceptical sociologist would probably not be totally convinced that all the clusters make sense, but willing to admit, that there might be something in them.

Are the correlations between grades in the same cluster positive? The first, empirical, cluster has 16 values with 120 intercorrelations, 113 of them positive. The second, social, cluster has 3 values with 3 intercorrelations, all positive and the third, theoretical, cluster has 7 values with 21 intercorrelations, all positive. Well, so far so good, although it would of course be easy to cut down clusters in order to get rid of negative correlations. But that would then cut back and give us a number of positive correlations between variables from *different* clusters. So let us have a look at them before we make too much of the positive correlations within the *same* cluster.

The empirical cluster has 192 correlations with variables from other clusters, that should be negative: 132 are so. The social theoretical cluster has 75 correlations with other clusters: 52 are negative as they should. The theoretical cluster has 147 correlations with other clusters: 124 are negative. The small cluster of value 24, additional information, had 16 out of its 27 correlations negative and value 27, number of pages, had 20 negative out of 27. Thus negative correlations certainly dominated, but there was a number of positive correlations. That could be taken as an indication that these theses varied more in their resources than we want them to do, making the interclass correlations stronger and thus lowering the negative correlations between variables from different clusters and making some correlations positive.

The matrix thus gives a total picture of the research process that can be summarized this way: Most Ph.D. candidates try to take care of empirical values, although some go in for social (or rather administrative) values instead. One candidate remained committed to theoretical values. If the authors, however, feel that they should try to compensate for value grades which have not come up to their expectations, they either throw in additional information nobody has asked for (value 24) or broaden their views over a large number of pages (value 27).

In our opinion the matrix speaks in favor of the summation theory. There are rather evident clusters which make sense and behave up to point as we expected them to do. Then we should be able to take one step further and try to study the importance of the different values.

The Importance of Values

A Swedish Ph.D. candidate has to print his thesis, hand over about 300 copies to the Academic authorities, give the faculty opponent three weeks to go through the thesis and then stand the official trial, where the opponents thoroughly go through his work before the faculty members. A small committee suggests what mark should be given the thesis, but the faculty pays much attention to these things and high marks are given grudgingly. Different faculties might follow slightly different norms, but probably these differences are rather small. The mark given the thesis by the faculty should be useful as an overall evaluation of its scientific value sum. We use this mark as criterion for computing the *criterion importance* of our 29 (or really 28) scientific values.

The stronger effect, that is, the stronger correlation a value's grades have with the marks, the higher criterion importance has the value. The correlations of the value grades with the mark are given in the third line from the bottom in the matrix (31 mark).

The correlations are there, of course, and they vary from $+1.00$ to -1.00. It certainly should be easy to rank our scientific values according to these correlations. Is it possible to test the mark some way, get a kind of validation criterion for our criterion? Well, if somebody asked us to mark the theses, we would of course use the sum of the theses' grades as our mark and this variable has a correlation with the marks +.62, acceptable but not very high.

But how has for instance news value (no. 12) got a correlation of +1.00 with marks? Because the five theses with most news value (grade 3 actually) all had marks above the mean. And how have the four theoretical values 7–10 got bottom correlations −1.00? Because the single thesis paying attention to these values was not considered fit for honour's degree. Evidently it is a bit risky to base our measure of importance on so varying conditions. It seems especially unsound to let the highly unstable data from the theoretical cluster influence the somewhat more stable data from the empirical and the social cluster. One way out of this—if we insist on measuring the values' importance—is to let each cluster of values have a rank order of its own.

We have then the second possibility to measure the importance by using the mean of the correlations of a value grade scale with all the variables belonging to other clusters. We have given these interaction weights in the bottom row of the matrix. These weights turn out to vary between +1.00 and −.07. But a look at the row shows that we have just as good reasons to make the rank order of these weights for one cluster at the time. Actually these mean correlations are just as unstable in the theoretical cluster as we previously found the criterion importance to be.

But we have not taken into account the simplest measure of importance that most sociologists would jump at: the mean of the grades. If a value is very important, then of course it has to reach a high grade. Well, that is true, but how do we know if a grade is high or low? We have after all only a grade scale and no possibility to judge whether a certain thesis has reached the "important" grade or not. Of course our scales reflect our own ideas of important grades, but how general are these ideas then? We do not know. Still, there is a chance that we have intuitively come off rather well. Well, we can try the means too, then, as a last column, although most of the grade scales have five steps, some have 3, 4, 6, or more. The 3-step grade scales we handle by naming the grades 1, 3, and 5, the grades of pages (value 27) we here cut down from seven to four actually used.

Let us start with the empirical cluster and its 16 scientific values. We rank them according to their criterion importance (that is, their correlation with marks), then give their correlation with the sum of value grades, the interaction weights (mean correlations with variables in other clusters,

Table 2. *Scientific values from the empirical cluster of Ph.D. theses, in rank order of their criterion importance. Their correlations with grade sum and their interaction weights are also given*

No.	Value	1. Criterion importance	2. Correlation with grade sum	3. Interaction weights	4. Grade means	5. Mean rank of 1, 3 and 4
16	Statistical model	+1.00⎤	+1.00	+.37	1.4	6.7
12	News value	+1.00⎦	+ .57	+.29	2.2	8.8
23	Fate of hypothesis	+ .81	+ .39	+.31	1.8	9.2
14	Variables' definition	+ .74⎤	+ .96	+.21	3.7	7.3
19	Analysis method	+ .74⎦	+ .83	+.40	2.5	4.8
20	Mathematical treatment	+ .70	+ .64	+.22	2.9	8.8
15	Mathematical model	+ .68⎤	+1.00	+.36	1.9	8.2
2	Reliability	+ .68⎦	+1.00	+.34	3.6	5.7
5	Generalization	+ .65	+ .91	+.33	3.2	7.0
3	Validity	+ .61	+ .74	+.27	2.4	11.5
18	Scale's actuality	+ .56	+ .65	+.30	1.8	12.3
25	References	+ .50⎤	+ .62	+.37	2.6	7.5
22	Non-response	+ .50⎦	+ .36	+.35	3.7	6.3
1	Presentation of hypothesis	+ .48	+ .86	+.34	2.9	8.7
17	Scales	+ .46	+ .55	+.32	2.4	11.5
6	Theory	+ .27	+ .86	+.30	2.6	11.7

sign changed) and at last the mean of the grades. This rank list is given in Table 2.

We must admit that these four measures, 1–4, seem to have rather little in common although all of them can be said to measure "importance" in some sense. Take for instance value 16, statistical model. The data suggest that this value seldom reaches a high grade (mean is low), but a good grade means a high mark and also a good interaction weight. Value 16, reliability, has a middle sized criterion importance, but is taken care of (grade mean next highest) and has a high interaction weight, being able to compensate deficiencies in other values. Value 6, theory, has the lowest criterion importance, it means little for the mark, but has a mean grade near the middle and an interaction weight a little below. Actually all these "importance" measures seem to make some sense although they measure different aspects of a complicated reality we were imprudent enough to construct as a unidimenstional variable just by calling it: "importance". As if this could give us a guarantee not only for the existence of this variable but also for a convenient measure of it.

Sociologists are generally eager to make their measures as "pure" as possible, but when they use them for prediction they often go to the opposite extreme and try to combine all the aspects into one single scale. We might do so in this case also by just adding the three ranks each

Table 3. *Scientific values of the social cluster in rank order of their criterion impor-tance. Their correlations with grade sum, their interaction weight, and their mean rank are also given*

No.	Value	1. Criterion importance	2. Correlation with grade sum	3. Interaction weights	4. Grade means	5. Mean rank of 1, 3 and 4
4	Sampling	+.81	+.09	.11	3.3	2
11	Usefulness to society	+.39	−.36	.18	2.6	2.3
21	Material's size	+.09	−.62	.32	4.4	1.7

Table 4. *Scientific values of the theoretical cluster of the Ph.D. sample in rank order of their criterion importance. Their correlations with grade sum, their interaction weight, and their rank are also given.*

No.	Value	1. Criterion importance	2. Correlation with grade sum	3. Interaction weights	4. Grade means	5. Mean rank of 1, 3 and 4
26	Language	+ .27	+ .65	− .12	3.1	3.0
13	School's usefulness	− .48	+ .26	+ .15	2.0	3.3
29	Disguise of defects	− .62	− .22	− .07	2.7	3.7
10	Variable construction	−1.00	−1.00	+1.00	1.3	4.0
7	Theory construction	−1.00	−1.00	+1.00	1.2	4.7
8	Hypothesis construction	−1.00	−1.00	+1.00	1.2	4.7
9	Model construction	−1.00	−1.00	+1.00	1.2	4.7

value has got on criterion importance, interaction weight, and grade mean. Value no. 16 statistical model for instance would get $1.5 + 2.5 + 16; 20: 3 = 6.7$. We give these composite importance measures here in or-der to see if they have any tendency to return in about the same rank order in other samples. If they do not, we have wasted our time and taken unnecessary risks, as ranks should not be added this way.

Let us then turn to the second cluster, that of social scientific values. The same rank list for these three values is given in Table 3.

The different measures of importance certainly do differ in this cluster too. A large thesis for instance does not pay in marks but still has a high grade mean and rather good interaction weight. Good sampling on the other hand is well paid in marks but few theses attend to it (grade means middle sized) and its ability to compensate or be compensated is low.

The third, theoretical cluster has seven scientific values in it, which can be seen in Table 4.

Here the pattern at least is easy to explain. The one theoretical thesis has a mark below the median and thus all the first six planning values are empirical and correlate -1.00 with mark. On the other hand this thesis can be said to compensate them by theoretical values which then get a maximum interaction weight of $+1.00$. If our single theoretical thesis had a mark above the median, there would evidently have been a perfect agreement between criterion importance and interaction weight —which shows how unstable our measures are in a sample like this.

The two remaining small clusters have just one value each and there is nothing to gain—for the moment—from taking in their values too. We can, however, return to them later on.

On the whole we have got little out of our exertions trying to measure importance. Still, we might have more success with other materials.

The interaction between scientific values in a sample of M.A. theses

We have found some interesting things in the matrix of the intercorrelations between grades of scientific values presented in Swedish Ph.D. theses, but we did not get much out of our attempts to measure the importance of the values. We would then come in a far better position if we could point out strong similarities ("invariances") between matrices from different samples. The M.A. theses could be taken next.

But of course we must first point out how M.A. theses differ from Ph.D. theses. And besides, we were not able to secure all Swedish M.A. theses, only those presented at the sociological department at the University of Stockholm and even in this set some theses escaped us (having disappeared from the shelves). The first difference then is that our sample of M.A. theses represents the value system of Stockholm sociologists and pays far less attention to value systems related to the sociological departments in Uppsala, Lund, and Gothenburg (Umeå not yet producing M.A. theses). Theoretically this ought to weaken the compensation pattern in the matrix, as it is no longer possible to use Stockholm values to compensate for lack of Uppsala, Lund, or Gothenburg values.

The second difference would be a tendency for lower grades of scientific values at the M.A. level. M.A. theses are preliminary to Ph.D. work, take shorter time, use far less resources, etc.

The third difference is that Ph.D. theses are publicly discussed at the dissertation, while M.A. theses are held for three weeks but in practice marked only by the professor. His private whims or weaknesses thus mean far more for M.A. theses than for Ph.D. theses.

The scientific value 28, value of researcher's title (degree), will be just as useless for M.A. theses as for Ph.D. theses. Otherwise we should be able to use the same variables, and thus need not present them once more. The list of the scales is given in the appendix.

The 28 values are placed in the order that makes most out of of the clusters we are waiting for. In Matrix 2 we can see how our own expectations fare when confronted with empirical evidence (value 23, fate of hypothesis).

Here we find the empirical cluster with 16 values although two of the set from the Ph.D. theses (no. 19, analysis method and no. 25, number of references) have been exchanged for no. 4, sampling, and no. 21, material's size. The social cluster has no counterpart among the M.A. theses, which might mean that official agencies accept doctors' theses but are less enthusiastic about M.A. theses. But the theoretical cluster has returned with a set of six values, the four construction values 7, 8, 9, and 10 this time connected with the values 11, usefulness to society and 19, analysis method. The six remaining values are paired off as three 2-value clusters of additional values (only 13, school's usefulness is not but a planning value instead). We discuss the clusters in the order of the matrix.

The empirical cluster contains seven planning values and nine working values, no additional values. This certainly makes sense, although it is a bit disturbing, that value 19, analysis method, should not be included in this cluster, but in the theoretical one. The 16 values have 120 inter-correlations between their grades, 94 of them positive, and 192 correlations with grades for values in other clusters, only 119 of them negative.

The theoretical cluster contains five theoretical values and one working value, no. 19, analysis method. But the foundation for this cluster is just as unstable in our sample of M.A. theses as previously in the sample of Ph.D. theses: once more a single thesis that this time happened to take care of the values 11 and 19, instead of 13, 26, and 29. Data for this cluster evidently should not be taken very seriously. The six values have, however, 15 intercorrelations between their grades that should be positive and are so in all cases, and then 132 correlations with grades for the values in other clusters that should be negative; they are so in 88 cases.

Then we have the remaining three small clusters of additional values that easily can be used to compensate grades that have been reduced or left out.

Value 13, school's usefulness, and 27, number of pages, are strongly correlated with one another. Only 30 of their 52 correlations with values from other clusters are negative.

Value 24, additional information, and 26, language, are of course positively correlated, or they would not have been brought together in the same cluster, 37 of their 52 correlations with other clusters are negative.

Value 25, number of references, and 29, disguise of defects are correlated yes, and 35 of their 52 correlations with grades in other value clusters negative.

This total picture still makes sense although it places the responsible professor, Boalt, in a somewhat ridiculous light. The M.A. candidates of his department seem to go in for empirical values and in one single case for theoretical values. But if at the end of their research they find themselves too far below their level of aspiration they mobilize as many additional values as they need. In the first run they rise the summation theory (13 school's usefulness, placed as a planning value, as we did not suspect this use of our summation theory in advance) and then prepare many pages about few points. In the second run they try giving additional information nobody has asked for and have the thing elegantly wrapped up in a foreign language. In the last run they can roll themselves in a large number of references and try to pass by the worst deficiencies. Thus, we have actually no need for negative correlations between the three last small clusters. They can be used either alone or together in any combination.

We could then try to handle all the small clusters acting as last minute compensation values as a single cluster. This cluster then would have six values with 15 intercorrelations that need not in this case necessarily be positive, although we prefer positive correlations to negative ones. Actually 9 out of the 15 are positive. The six values have 132 correlations with the two previous clusters (the empirical one and the theoretical) that should be negative; 96 actually are so.

The M.A. candidates seem to have used these additional values far more efficiently than we expected—or the professor responsible for letting them through was far more naïve than he himself realized.

The importance of values in a sample of M.A. theses

This time we use only two measures of importance: criterion importance and interaction weight. Our main point now is not to compare these two measures, as they seem to measure different things but to compare the rank orders of the values in Ph.D. theses with M.A. theses, cluster for cluster. Do they give similar pictures, and if not, how can we explain the differences.

But to make these comparisons between the same clusters in the two different samples measuring full, both clusters must contain the same set of values. We can attain that either by simply deciding what common set of values should be used in both (and all other) samples—which might be difficult to justify—or by excluding values that are not included in both of the corresponding clusters. The latter way of course is the easier and so we take that.

We must then start giving the importance rank data for the M.A. theses matrix alone and then cut down the list of values to the common core in order to compare importance of Ph.D. values with M.A. values. We do this cluster for cluster and start with the empirical one, given in Table 5.

Value 16, statistical model and 14, variables' definitions, seem to be so important for a good mark and so well taken care of that they hardly can be compensated by other values, and thus get low interaction weights. It is no coincidence that value 6, problem's integration with theory, stands at the bottom. This value was, sad to say, intentionally sidestepped for many years at the Stockholm department and the result is that it was not very useful even for compensation purposes.

The two values, 4, sampling, and 21, material's size, which have been included in this cluster here, but not in the Ph.D. sample, have little criterion importance, but the size of material turns out to be very useful as a compensation for lack of other value grades.

In Table 6 is given the comparison of the fourteen variables belonging to the empirical clusters in both our samples of theses. We compare only criterion importance, correlation with grade sum, and interaction weight.

There is a rather good consensus between the rank orders of these values in criterion importance (rank order correlation $+.44$) and also in correlation with grade sum. But there is a negative correlation $(-.54)$ between the ranks of interaction weights.

In Table 7 the same pattern returns again in the theoretical cluster of

56

Table 5. *Scientific values from the empirical cluster of M.A. theses, in rank order of their criterion importance. Their correlations with grade sums and their interaction weights are also given.*

No.	Value	Criterion importance	Correlation with grade sum	Interaction weight
16	Statistical model	1.00	1.00	−.19
14	Variables' definition	.62	.86	.04
12	News value	.52	.13	.36
18	Scale's actuality	.35	.56	.10
17	Scales	.26	.63	.14
3	Validity	.17	.33	.24
20	Mathematical treatment	.15	.60	.17
22	Non-response	.12	.74	.07
2	Reliability	.12	.15	.05
5	Generalization	.07	.63	.10
4	Sampling	−.07	.30	.10
21	Material's size	−.08	.08	.50
1	Presentation of hypotheses	−.12	.60	.21
15	Mathematical model	−.13	.51	−.11
23	Fate of hypotheses	−.17	−.07	.10
6	Theory	−.27	.49	.22

Table 6. *Scientific values from the empirical clusters of Ph.D. and M.A. theses in rank order of their criterion importance in Ph.D. samples. Their correlations with grade sums and their interaction weights are also given*

No.	Value	Criterion importance		Correlation with grade sum		Interaction weights	
		Ph.D.	M.A.	Ph.D.	M.A.	Ph.D.	M.A.
16	Statistical model	1.00	1.00	1.00	1.00	.37	−.19
12	News value	1.00	.52	.57	.13	.29	.36
23	Fate of hypotheses	.81	−.17	.39	−.07	.31	.10
14	Variables' definition	.74	.62	.96	.86	.21	.04
20	Mathematical treatment	.70	.15	.64	.60	.22	.17
15	Mathematical model	.68	−.13	1.00	.51	.36	−.11
2	Reliability	.68	.12	1.00	.15	.34	.05
5	Generalization	.65	.07	.91	.63	.33	.10
3	Validity	.61	.17	.74	.33	.27	.24
18	Scale's actuality	.56	.35	.65	.56	.30	.10
22	Non-response	.50	.12	.36	.74	.35	.07
1	Presentation of hypotheses	.48	−.12	.86	.60	.34	.21
17	Scales	.46	.26	.55	.63	.32	.14
6	Theory	.27	−.27	.86	.49	.30	.22

this sample: criterion importance and correlation with grade sum give rank orders positively correlated with each, but both negatively correlated with the rank order of interaction weights.

57

Table 7. *Scientific values from the theoretical cluster of M.A. theses in rank order of their criterion importance. Their correlations with grade sum and their interaction weights are also given*

No.	Value	Criterion importance	Correlation with grade sum	Interaction weights
19	Analysis method	1.00	.60	− .24
8	Hypothesis construction	1.00	− .18	.22
9	Model construction	1.00	− .18	− .18
10	Variable construction	1.00	− .18	− .18
11	Usefulness to society	.42	.12	− .03
7	Theory construction	−1.00	−1.00	1.00

Table 8. *Scientific values from the theoretical clusters of Ph.D. and M.A. theses, in rank order of their criterion importance in Ph.D. sample. Their correlations with grade sums and interaction values are also given*

No.	Value	Criterion importance		Correlation with grade sum		Interaction weights	
		Ph.D.	M.A.	Ph.D.	M.A.	Ph.D.	M.A.
10	Variable construction	−1.00	+ 1.00	−1.00	− .18	+ 1.00	− .18
7	Theory construction	−1.00	−1.00	−1.00	−1.00	+ 1.00	+ 1.00
8	Hypothesis construction	−1.00	+ 1.00	−1.00	− .18	+ 1.00	+ .22
9	Model construction	−1.00	+ 1.00	−1.00	− .18	+ 1.00	− .18

Table 9. *Scientific values from the additional clusters of M.A. theses, in rank order of their criterion importance. Their correlations with grade sums and interaction values are also given*

No.	Value	Criterion importance	Correlation with grade sum	Interaction weight
13	School's usefulness	− .08	.08	.16
27	Number of pages	− .12	− .15	− .03
24	Additional information	− .24	1.00	.17
25	Number of references	− .34	− .24	.16
29	Disguise of defects	− .71	− .34	.12
26	Language	−1.00	− .18	.49

This table is up to a point explained by the fact that the single thesis (by the way, *not* by the author of the theoretical Ph.D. thesis) using the constructional values 8–10 happened to take some care also of values 11, usefulness to society and 19, analysis method, and got a good mark.

Table 10. *Five additional values in the rank order of their criterion importance in the Ph.D. sample, from Ph.D. and from M.A. samples. Their correlations with grade sums and interaction weights are also given*

No.	Value	Criterion importance		Correlation with grade sum		Interaction weights	
		Ph.D.	M.A.	Ph.D.	M.A.	Ph.D.	M.A.
25	Number of references	.50	− .34	.62	− .24	.37	.16
26	Language	.27	−1.00	.65	− .18	−.12	.49
24	Additional information	.06	− .24	.57	1.00	.15	.17
27	Number of pages	−.14	− .12	−.26	− .15	.15	−.03
29	Disguise of defects	−.62	− .71	−.22	− .34	−.22	.12

Then let us have a look at the four theoretical values turning up in both samples (Table 8).

There is not much here as the table is the result of one single theoretical Ph.D. thesis taking care of values 7–10, getting a low mark, low grade sum, and not trying to cover other values, while the single theoretical M.A. thesis took only of values 8–10, got a high mark, a grade sum below the median, and tried to cover some other values.

The remaining three small clusters of additional values in the matrix of the M.A. values can easily be grasped out of the matrix itself. We previously mentioned that in one sense these additional values need not compete with each other. We are thus excused for handling them just as a single cluster, although they actually are three separate ones. And so this last, additional cluster can be accounted for in Table 9.

We have now at last the chance we have been waiting for, to find out how much these additional values actually help M.A. candidates. Value 13, making use of the professor's weakness for the summation theory (school's usefulness), evidently did a lot, giving correlations near zero with mark and grade sum, which might mean that grades here nearly filled the gaps that had to be compensated. Many pages were nearly as good for the mark as the summation theory, but the remaining additional values evidently did not fool the professor—at least not often. He is especially grateful for the strong negative correlation, − .71, between mark of thesis and value 29, disguise of defects—although we admit that if deficiences are cleverly disguised, he will not detect them.

Is there any sense in comparing additional values in the two samples? Well, we could exclude value 13, having a special bearing in the M.A. sample and compare the five remaining additional values 24, 25, 26, 27, and 29, assuming that they remain additional, that is, are used for compensation, whatever cluster they got into. The usual data about these five values in both samples are given in Table 10.

No pattern is visible to our eyes; the results thus do not encourage the point of view tested in this table. Our five additional values either do not function the same way in all samples or with very varying importance.

The total picture and the importance measures

We expected the M.A. matrix to show a less pronounced compensation pattern than the Ph.D. matrix, and it did: a lower percent of positive correlations within samples, a lower percent of negative correlations between the samples and—as a result of this—generally lower importance measures for the values.

We brought in our second sample because we hoped that this M.A. sample would give us the same set of clusters and the same rank order of the values' importance we had already found in the Ph.D. sample. Actually the two samples showed rather convincing similarities in cluster patterns. The social cluster from the Ph.D. sample did not turn up in the M.A. thesis, but the empirical as well as the theoretical cluster did and some additional clusters too. We realize that this only shows that sociologists try to reach a common core of important planning and working values (the empirical cluster), that some few go in for theoretical values instead (which gives this theoretical cluster a very instable basis) and that additional values are used to compensate serious losses of aspired grades.

As soon as we want to estimate the importance of these different values we are in difficulty partly because our two single theoretical theses play havoc with the correlations, driving them towards the extremes of $+1.00$ or -1.00, partly because our measures of importance seem to cover very different aspects. We thought that the grades of accepted scientific values would on the one side correlate with the mark of the thesis (and with the grade sum), and the important values would show their importance by attaining stronger correlations in all three cases. This, however, is not the case. Marks and grade sums tend to follow each other, but their rank orders have no correlations with rank orders of interaction weights (that is, mean correlation with grades from other clusters)—or strong negative ones.

We are thus forced to give up the idea of scientific value consensus. Some values might be generally accepted and given approximately the same weight, others might vary more or less in importance. Then we could use the grade's correlation with mark or possibly grade sum to measure criterion importance which ought to point out the heavier consensus values. The interaction weights on the other hand should give weight partly to those commonly held values that are well suited to compensate losses of aspired grades, partly values that are hopefully given much more weight by those using them than by those abstaining from them.

Nevertheless, how can we account for the fact that in the empirical cluster the sample of Ph.D. theses gave a rank order to the values according to their interaction weight that was reversed in the sample of M.A. theses (rank correlation −.54)? Well, if we have to suggest something, we could point to the fact that M.A. projects generally have much smaller resources available than the Ph.D. projects. The Ph.D. candidates have to stand a hard trial and in our opinion they tend to stack their resources on the values most useful for a high mark and probably most difficult to attain. The M.A. candidates usually have fewer resources and are anxious to reach a decent grade sum—and mark—all the same. The simplest way to do so would be to take as many easily attained values as possible and to abstain from the difficult ones, in spite of their impressive importance—unless there happens to be an excellent chance for getting them cheap. This deviating technique for selecting scientific values would neither upset correlations between marks and grades, nor change the rank order of criterion importance. But it would have some effect on the correlations between grades and grade sum and then eventually reverse the rank order of interaction weights, as the less heavy values used for compensation by the Ph.D. candidates tend to be more or less compulsory to the M.A. candidates, while they seldom can use as a successful compensation the difficult values that Ph.D. candidates must try to attain.

This explanation cannot be tested, and should not be taken too seriously. But evidently there could be reasons to distrust the interaction weight as an importance measure. Still—this measure does measure an aspect that has some interest to us. We should not abandon it, but be aware of the many risks connected with it.

We still need more experience of clusters and their interaction as the matrices show them. We need more samples, but then have to turn to articles in scientific journals and we have tried two of them.

CHAPTER 7

The Researcher's Role

Studied in American Sociological Review and Acta Sociologica and Compared to the Previous Samples

We wanted to study the interaction of scientific values not only in Ph.D. and M.A. theses, but also in articles from scientific journals, hoping to find similarities in cluster formation and in importance. We chose as journals *American Sociological Review* volume 26, year 1961 and *Acta Sociologica,* volumes 4, 5 and 6, the years 1960–1962, three years in order to get about the same number of articles as the one year of *American Sociological Review.*

We used our usual scales for measuring scientific values grades on the 55 articles in volume 26 of *American Sociological Review.* The scales of nr 13 (research school's usefulness) and 26 (language) had to be given up, as we had no chance to estimate value 13 on the American scene and as all articles were in English. So we are left with 27 scientific values and the sum of their scores.

Interaction between the scientific value scores in American Sociological Review

We hoped of course that the general picture of the interaction in Ph.D. and M.A. theses would be found in the *American Sociological Review.* Some Swedish values might turn out irrelevant in the United States and vice versa, but the general trend should be the same: an empirical cluster, a theoretical cluster and one or more additional clusters compensating one another in the sense that grades from one cluster tend to have positive correlations within the same cluster but negative correlations with grades from other clusters. That is, the set of values might vary a little between Sweden and the United States, but the general reaction pattern of the sociologists should remain the same.

The correlations between the grades are as usually presented in a matrix, and this matrix (Matrix 3) to our joy gives *one empirical cluster* of sixteen values, all of them planning values or working values, *one theoretical cluster* of eight values including the four constructive planning values but also three additional values and a third cluster, dominated by the additional value 25, number of references, (in the sense that this variable gives higher correlations) but also containing two planning values, no. 6, theory, and no. 12, news value. This last piece is not quite what we expected, but still not a very serious thing. The main pattern still holds, and the clusters come out quite clearly. The empirical cluster has 16 values, thus 120 intercorrelations and 112 of them positive. The 176 correlations with grades from other clusters are negative in 141 cases. The corresponding correlations for the theoretical cluster's eight values are 23 positive intercorrelations out of 28 within the cluster, and 115 negative correlations out of 152 correlations with other clusters. The third small cluster with only three values has all three intercorrelations positive, and 62 negative correlations out of the 72 correlations with other clusters.

We could of course try to analyze the importance measures here, but prefer to do so after first having had a look at all four samples, all four matrices and a discussion of their differences in values.

Interaction between the scientific value grades in *Acta Sociologica*

We could not use value 15 (mathematical model) in this case, as no article had such a model, but otherwise we use the same values as for the previous sample and in Matrix 4 we give their intercorrelations from the 55 articles in the usual matrix form.

The empirical cluster turns up with 18 values, 8 of them planning values, 9 working values and one an additional value, no. 24, additional information. *The theoretical cluster* has 7 values, the four usual construction values and 3 additional values. *The additional cluster* is just no. 25, number of references. This agrees with the total picture quite well.

All of these three clusters come out clearly. The empirical cluster has 18 values, and thus 153 intercorrelations, 141 of which were positive.

Table 11. *Proportion positive correlations within the clusters and negative correlations between the clusters in the four samples*

Sample	Proportion of positive correlations within clusters	Proportion of negative correlations between clusters	Number of clusters
Ph.D. theses	93 %	73 %	5
M.A. theses	81 %	70 %	5
American Sociological Review	91 %	80 %	3
Acta Sociologica	92 %	77 %	3

The 144 correlations with other clusters were negative in 114 cases. The theoretical cluster had seven values and so 21 intercorrelations, all but 2 positive. The 133 correlations with other clusters were negative in 96 cases. The last little cluster had only one value and 22 negative (or zero) correlations out of 25.

How clear cut are the clusters in our four samples?

We can get an overall picture by computing for each sample the proportion of positive correlations within the clusters and the proportion of negative correlations between the clusters. We have to keep in mind that the sample of M.A. theses is taken only from Stockholm, which should reduce its tendency to form clusters, as in this case different departments with different sets of values no longer compete with each other. The general tendencies can be seen in Table 11.

The M.A. theses—as we expected—show a weaker tendency of clustering. We next take a look at the four clusters we have labeled as empirical, theoretical, social and additional. The social cluster turned up only in the Ph.D. sample. Let us begin with the empirical cluster, registering all values included in this cluster at least in the matrix of one sample, giving at the same time their *importance,* measured by the grade sum criterion or the interaction weight. An empty cell means of course that the value in this case was included in some other cluster.

An analysis of the empirical cluster

Table 12 demonstrates that out of the 20 values included here (no. 15 included although it was useless in the journal samples) eleven appeared

Table 12. Criterion importance and interaction weights of the values in the empirical cluster of the four samples

	Criterion importance (criterion: grade sum)								Interaction weights							
	Correlation				Rank order				Mean correlation				Rank order			
Value	Ph.D.	M.A.	A.S.R.	Acta	Ph.D.	M.A.	A.S.R.	Acta	Ph.D.	M.A.	A.S.R.	Acta	Ph.D.	M.A.	A.S.R.	Acta
1 Presentation of hypothesis	+.86	+.60	+.78	+.83	5.5	6.5	11	12.5	+.34	+.21	+.16	+.49	6.5	6	11.5	15
2 Reliability	+1.00	+.15	+.71	+.93	2	13	15	7	+.34	+.05	+.52	+.50	6.5	14	3	13.5
3 Validity	+.74	+.33	+.75	+1.00	9	11	12	3	+.27	+.24	+.67	+.67	14	4	1	2
4 Sampling	—	+.30	+.96	+.91	—	12	4.5	9	—	+.10	+.24	+.62	—	10.5	9	6
5 Generalization	+.91	+.63	+1.00	+.54	5	4.5	2	17.5	+.33	+.10	+.56	+.82	8	10.5	2	1
6 Theory	+.86	+.49	—	+.87	6.5	10	—	10	+.30	+.21	—	+.17	11.5	5	—	17
11 Usefulness to society	—	—	+.32	+.54	—	—	16	17.5	—	—	+.10	-.03	—	—	14.5	18
12 News value	+.57	+.13	—	+.58	13	14	—	16	+.29	+.36	—	+.28	13	2	—	16
14 Variables' definition	+.96	+.86	+1.00	+.93	4	2	2	7	+.21	+.34	+.31	+.55	15	3	7	8.5
15 Mathematical model	+1.00	+.51	(+)	(+)	2	9	—	—	+.36	-.11	(+)	(+)	4	15	(+)	—
16 Statistical model	+1.00	+1.00	+1.00	+1.00	2	1	2	3	+.37	-.19	-.02	+.50	2.5	16	16	13.5
17 Scales	+.55	+.63	+.84	+1.00	1.4	4.5	8.5	3	+.32	+.14	+.48	+.62	9	8	4	6
18 Scales' actuality	+.55	+.56	+.89	+1.00	10	8	6	3	+.30	+.10	+.46	+.63	11.5	10.5	5.5	4
19 Analysis method	+.83	—	+.84	+.93	8	—	8.5	7	+.40	—	+.17	+.55	1	—	10	8.5
20 Mathematical method	+.64	+.60	+.81	—	11	6.5	10	—	+.22	+.17	+.16	—	15	7	11.5	3
21 Material's size	—	+.08	+.74	+.86	—	15	13.5	15	—	+.50	+.27	+.66	—	1	8	10
22 Non-response	+.36	+.74	+.74	+.83	16	3	13.5	11	+.35	+.07	+.10	+.54	5	13	14.5	6
23 Fate of hypotheses	+.39	-.07	+.88	+.73	15	16	7	12.5	+.31	+.10	+.12	+.62	10	10.5	13	11
24 Additional information	—	—	+.96	+1.00	—	—	4.5	14	—	—	+.46	+.53	—	—	5.5	12
25 References	+.62	+.96	—	—	12	—	—	3	+.37	—	—	+.51	2.5	—	—	—

Table 13. *Presence in the four samples and grade means for the 19 values in the empirical cluster. Means for excluded values between brackets*

No.	Value	Present in sample of				Mean of grades in sample of			
		Ph.D.	M.A.	Am. Soc. Rev.	Acta	Ph.D.	M.A.	Am. Soc. Rev.	Acta
1	Presentation of hypotheses	+	+	+	+	2.76	2.75	2.45	2.12
2	Reliability	+	+	+	+	3.38	3.21	2.31	2.14
3	Validity	+	+	+	+	2.57	2.32	1.47	1.36
4	Sampling	−	+	+	+	(3.10)	3.71	2.78	2.18
5	Generalization	+	+	+	+	3.10	2.64	1.15	1.40
6	Theory	+	+	−	+	2.48	2.04	(3.42)	2.38
11	Usefulness to society	−	−	+	+	(2.52)	(2.11)	2.22	1.52
12	News value	+	+	−	+	2.10	2.11	(2.25)	2.08
14	Variables' definition	+	+	+	+	3.52	3.36	2.45	2.22
15	Mathematical model	+	+	+	+	1.81	1.32	1.11	1.06
16	Statistical model	+	+	+	+	1.33	1.32	1.11	1.06
17	Scales	+	+	+	+	2.24	1.93	1.75	1.42
18	Scales' actuality	+	+	+	+	1.76	1.75	1.53	1.32
19	Analysis method	+	−	+	+	2.38	(2.82)	2.40	2.04
20	Mathematical model	+	+	+	+	2.76	2.71	2.22	1.48
21	Material's size	−	+	+	+	(4.14)	4.04	2.78	2.76
22	Non-response	+	+	+	+	3.62	4.14	2.31	2.22
23	Fate of hypothesis	+	+	+	+	1.76	2.29	2.78	2.38
24	Additional information	−	−	+	+	(1.38)	(1.43)	1.63	1.20
25	References	+	−	−	−	6.48	(3.89)	(4.05)	(3.26)

in all four samples, six in three of them, two in two samples and one in just one sample. There is evidently a tendency to remain in the same cluster.

The rank orders of the criterion importance seem to be acceptable but the interaction weights are less reliable and evidently not possible to use in this context.

Criterion importance then seems to be unanimously given to value 16, statistical model, value 14, variable's definition, and possibly value 18, scales' actuality. Low rank seems to be given value 11, usefulness to society, value 12, news value, and value 21, material's size.

Before we leave our experimental cluster, we ought however, to look also at the mean grades of the values in the four samples. The set of scientific values we use probably suits the Swedish Ph.D. dissertations so *they* ought to get the highest grade sums, M.A. theses should be considerably lower. The two journals probably use somewhat deviant sets of values and so should present lower grade sums. *American Socio-*

logical Review on the one hand should have a higher scientific standard, and on the other hand be less dependent of Swedish articles. The mean grade sums, however, come out this way:

	Mean Grade Sum
Ph.D. theses	75.7
M.A. theses	65.8
American Sociological Review	60.1
Acta Sociologica	53.3

When we now intend to present the grade means for our empirical values in each of our four samples, we thus have reasons to expect that these means will be highest in the Ph.D. theses and successively lower in M.A. theses, articles from *American Sociological Review* and lowest in *Acta Sociologica*. Yes, they should be, unless the researchers in a special sample paid much more or much less attention to the value than the researchers in the other samples. The more attention, the higher should the mean be.

One simple way of pointing out samples of disagreeing researchers is the table showing which values are included in the empirical cluster. If a sample excludes a value, present in all the others, there is evidently a disagreement.

We then intend to give for each value out of the empirical cluster the four means from the four samples and expect them to fall from the Ph.D. sample all the way down to the *Acta Sociologica* sample, *unless* one or more of the samples have excluded the value from this cluster.

In Table 13 we take the 20 values and first indicate their presence or absence in each of the four samples, then their means of each value's grades. The means for the grades of the excluded values are between brackets to point them out.

There are 12 values represented in all four samples, nine of them indicate the consistent decline from Ph.D. sample down to *Acta* sample we expect, three of them do not. There are 8 values not represented in all for samples, only one of the lines shows a consistent decline; the remaining seven do not. We thus construct the following four fold table:

	The fall of means is	
	Straight	Broken
Value not present in all samples	1	7
Value present in all samples	9	3

The table indicates a strong tendency for the values, represented in the empirical cluster of all samples, to decline consistently while those lacking in one or more samples clearly deviate from this role. Researchers who

Table 14. *Presence, grade means, criterion importance and interaction weights in the empirical cluster of all four samples*

No. Value	Presence in cluster				Mean of grade				Criterion importance				Interaction weights			
	Ph.D.	M.A.	A.S.R.	Acta	Ph.D.	M.A.	A.S.R.	Acta	Ph.D.	M.A.	A.S.R.	Acta	Ph.D.	M.A.	A.S.R.	Acta
1 Presentations of hypotheses	+	+	+	+	2.76	2.75	2.45	2.12	.86	.60	.78	.83	.34	.21	.16	.49
2 Reliability	+	+	+	+	3.38	3.21	2.31	2.14	1.00	.15	.71	.93	.34	.05	.52	.50
3 Validity	+	+	+	+	2.57	2.32	1.47	1.36	.74	.33	.75	1.00	.27	.24	.67	.67
4 Sampling	−	+	+	+	3.10[4]	3.71[1]	2.78	2.18	.09[4]	.30[1]	.96	.91	.11[4]	.10[1]	.24	.62
5 Generalization	+	+	+	+	3.10	2.64	1.15	1.40	.91	.63	.97	.54	.33	.10	.56	.82[1]
6 Theory	+	+	−	+	2.48	2.04[3]	3.42[4]	2.38	.86	.49[3]	.02[4]	.87	.30	.22[3]	.10[4]	.17
11 Usefulness to society	−	−	+	+	2.52[4]	2.11[4]	2.22[1]	1.52	−.36[4]	.12[4]	.32[1]	.54	.18[4]	−.03[4]	.10[1]	−.03
12 News value	+	+	−	+	2.10[3]	2.11[3]	2.25[4]	2.08	.57[3]	.13[3]	−.20[4]	.58	.29[3]	.36[3]	.39[4]	.28
14 Variables' definition	+	+	+	+	3.52	3.36	2.45	2.22	.96	.86	1.00	.93	.21	.04	.31	.55
15 Mathematical model	+	+	−	−	1.81	1.61	1.05[4]	1.00[4]	1.00	.51	±0[4]	±0[4]	.36	−.11	−.18[4]	±0[4]
16 Statistical model	+	+	+	+	1.33	1.32	1.11	1.06	1.00	1.00	1.00	1.00	.37	−.19	−.02	.50
17 Scales	+	+	+	+	2.24	1.93	1.75	1.42	.55	.63	.84	1.00	.32	.14	.48	.62
18 Scale's actuality	+	+	+	+	1.76	1.75	1.53	1.32	.65	.56	.89	1.00	.30	.10	.46	.63
19 Analysis method	+	−	+	+	2.38[3]	2.82[4]	2.40	2.04	.83[3]	.60[4]	.84	.93	.40[3]	−.24[4]	.17	.55
20 Mathematical method	+	+	+	+	2.76	2.71	2.22	1.48	.64	.60	.81	.59	.22	.17	.16	.66
21 Material's size	−	+	+	+	4.14[4]	4.04	2.78	2.76	.62[4]	.08	.74	.86	.32[4]	.50	.27	.54
22 Non-response	+	+	+	+	3.62[3]	4.14[1]	2.31	2.22	.36[3]	74[1]	.74	.83	.35[3]	.07[1]	.10	.62
23 Fate of response																

| 24 | Additional informa- tion | − | + | + | 1.38[4] | 1.43[4] | 1.53 | 1.20 | .57[4] | 1.00[4] | .96 | 1.00 | .15[4] | .17[4] | .46 | .51 |
| 25 | References + | − | − | − | 6.48 | 3.89[4] | 4.05[4] | 3.26[4] | .62 | −.24[4] | −.55[4] | −.25[4] | .37 | .16[4] | .52[4] | .11[4] |

[1] The mean is higher than the preceding mean.
[2] The mean answers our expectations (should be used for all means without number).
[3] The mean is lower than the following mean.
[4] The value grade has been taken out of the empirical cluster.

look at a value otherwise than the researchers in the other samples not only pay more (or less) attention to it, they also use it in another way, place it in another cluster.

Comparing the expected means of grades can thus give us methods to study the importance of the scientific values.

Interaction between means of grades and criterion importance in the empirical cluster

We know that the Ph.D. theses tend to have the highest grade sums, followed by the M.A. theses, the *American Sociological Review* articles and the *Acta Sociologica* articles in this order. We can thus expect that this order should tend to hold not only for the grade sums but also for each value grade making up this sum, unless a value for some reason has another weight and/or use for the researchers in a deviating sample. We can then use the expected decrease in grade means to point out samples and means that break the decrease expectation. Evidently there are three ways to break the role of decreasing grade means:

(1) The grade mean is so high that it surpasses the preceding mean, which is against our expectation.
(2) The grade mean is so low that it does not surpass the following value.
(3) The value grade has been pushed out of the empirical cluster.

If researchers in a sample of publications pay so much attention to a value that its mean grade is above the preceding mean grade, then we expect it to be given *more* importance by them.

If researchers in a sample pay so little attention to a value, that its mean grade is below the following mean grade, we expect it to have *less* importance for them.

If a value grade has been excluded from the empirical cluster, it has weak or negative correlations with the majority of the grade scales making up the grade sums and so should have *little* importance.

If a value grade happens to behave according to our expectations (giving a continuous decrease) it should have about the *same* importance as in the other samples of that value grade.

We can thus order the values included at some time in the empirical cluster, look at their grade means to point out the importance coefficients for each value and eventually the interaction weights in the same way.

Table 15. *Data on the criterion importance of the empirical cluster for the four samples*

		Ph.D. Importance		M.A. Importance		Am. Soc. Rev. Importance		Acta Importance		Sum Importance	
		<.70	>.70	<.55	>.55	<.80	>.80	<.90	>.90	<	>
1	Higher importance expected	0	0	1	1	0	2	0	0	1	3
2	Medium importance expected	4	8	4	7	6	7	8	9	22	31
3	Lower importance expected	3	1	3	0	0	1	0	0	6	2
4	Cluster changed, low importance	4	0	2	2	4	0	3	0	13	2

< indicates values below the median.
> indicates values above the median.

We have earmarked means, importance coefficients and interaction weights 1, 2, 3, 4 according to the following principles:

(1) Used for the cases where the mean is higher than the preceding mean, that is, given more weight, which should probably give also higher importance and interaction weight.

(2) Was meant to be used for the cases where the mean grades satisfy our expectations. These are, however, so many that the tables are more easily read without them. All cases not earmarked are thus 2. We expect these values to have about the same importance-interaction weight as the other samples of the value grade.

(3) Used for the cases where the mean is lower than the following mean. This indicates that the publications in this sample pay less attention to the grade and that importance-interaction weight ought to be lower than in the other corresponding samples.

(4) Used when the value grade in a sample has been excluded from the empirical cluster because of too few positive correlations with the other value grades within it. As the value grades of the empirical cluster dominate the grade sum, this probably should mean a low importance-interaction weight.

In Table 14 we present our data on the twenty possible scientific values present in the empirical cluster of at least one of the four samples.

If a mean is at the same time higher than the preceding mean and lower than the following, we look only at the direction where two means remain for comparison; for instance the mean of value 23 in the M.A.

theses has two values to the right and only one to the left and thus is handled as a mean lower than the following mean, although it also is higher than the preceding mean.

We sum up our data on the criterion importance in Table 15, one column for each sample and then a sum of them. See page 71.

The four different columns do not contradict our expectations and the sum of the four columns supports our hypothesis. When grade means are higher, the criterion importance also tends to be higher, where means are low, so tends importance to be. Cluster changing should be related to low importance, and so it is.

The grade means and the interaction weights in the empirical cluster

We have found, that after all criterion importance and interaction weight often point in different directions. In many cases we even expect them to do so. If for instance the researchers in one sample of publications pay far more attention to a value than the other researchers, we expect the criterion importance of this particular sample to *increase,* but the corresponding interaction to *decrease,* since the value has more attention paid to it and then is more dangerous to substitute with other values (this holds true only in the empirical cluster).

We try now to use this type of discussion, using the grade means of the four samples, the cluster and sometimes the criterion importance to predict which combinations of them should lead to a high *interaction weight* of the sample and which should lead to a low. We use the same classification of grade means and of high–low criterion importance as in our analysis of the criterion importance in the empirical cluster. Paying attention to the size of the criterion importance only when we handle the difficult case of a mean on the level we expect it to be—lower than the preceding mean or higher than the following—we get the following five categories:

(1) Mean too high, making it dangerous not to pay attention to it or to substitute it with grades of other values. Compensation weight ought to be low.

(2) a. Mean right, criterion importance high, indicating that the value can be profitably used to compensate other values. Compensation weight then expected to be high.

(2) b. Mean right, criterion importance low, indicating that the value cannot profitably be used for compensation, nor needs to be compensated. Compensation weight expected to be low.

(3) Mean too low, showing that the value is not paid attention to and so it should be less useful for compensation purposes. Compensation weight should be low.

(4) Value not present in the empirical cluster, but probably leaving some positive correlations with empirical values, resulting in low weight. Compensation weight then should be low.

The compensation weights are divided in high and low within each sample, the dividing line as near the median as possible: in the Ph.D. sample line at $+.32$, in M.A. $+.11$, in *American Sociological Review* at $+.25$ and in *Acta Sociologica* at $+.54$.

We use the same large table as previously to test the five expectations we have formulated. At the test they come out thus:

(1) Mean too high. Low compensation expected. Low in 4 cases of 5.

(2) a. Mean right, importance high. High compensation weight expected. High in 19 cases of 34.

(2) b. Mean right, importance low. Low compensation weight expected. Low in 12 cases of 22.

(3) Mean too low. Low compensation weight expected. Low in 7 cases of 11.

(4) Value not present. Low compensation weight expected. Low in 4 cases of 8.

All but the last row came out as we expected them. This, however, is due to the simple fact that in four cases of five we expect the weights to be low. If we had expected all five rows to be below the mean, this would clearly have been impossible. Four cases out of five are little better, but not quite impossible; as our results demonstrate.

An analysis of the theoretical cluster

We doubted from the start the usefulness of the theoretical cluster as its precarious existence hung on one single Ph.D. thesis and later on also on one single M.A. thesis. There are, however, two theoretically oriented articles in our sample from *American Sociological Review* and six from our sample out of *Acta Sociologica*. This is no overwhelming

Table 16. *Criterion importance and interaction weights of the values in the theoretical cluster of the four samples*

No.	Value	Criterion importance (criterion grade sum)				Interaction weights			
		Ph.D.	M.A.	Am. Soc. Rev.	Acta	Ph.D.	M.A.	Am. Soc. Rev.	Acta
7	Theory construction	−1.00	−1.00	−.04	−.40	+1.00	+1.00	+.42	+.85
8	Hypothesis construction	−1.00	−.18	−.04	−.40	+1.00	+.22	+.42	+.85
9	Model construction	−1.00	−.18	−.04	−.40	+1.00	−.18	+.42	+.85
10	Variable construction	−1.00	−.13	−1.00	+.19	+1.00	−.18	+.90	+.76
11	Usefulness to society	—	+.12	—	—	—	−.03	—	—
19	Analysis methods	—	+.60	—	—	—	−.24	—	—
27	Number of pages	—	—	+.02	−.01	—	—	+.11	+.07
29	Disguise of defects	−.22	—	−.28	+.10	−.07	—	+.26	+.52

evidence, but still enough to warrant the use of this cluster—if we so want. But it is evident that correlations and means will vary as the one publication—or the pair of them—happens to be graded. There is thus very little use to make any tables, but we present them all the same in Table 16. A lot of variables can however not be used here, as they have been irrelevant in one or more of the samples: 13, school's usefulness, 15, mathematical model, and 26, language, cannot be used for journals, 28, researcher's title, is useless for theses.

The grade means and the criterion importance in the theoretical cluster

As the empirical cluster dominates the values, it also dominates the grade sum, thus securing positive correlations between grade sum and empirical values—and negative correlations with the theoretical values. But on the other hand publications with good empirical grades have low theoretical grades and vice versa, which means that the theoretical values often get high interaction weights. These points could have been made in advance

Table 17. *Presence in the four samples and grade means for the values in the theoretical cluster. Means for excluded values between brackets*

No.	Value	Present in sample of				Mean of grades in sample of			
		Ph.D.	M.A.	Am. Soc. Rev.	Acta	Ph.D.	M.A.	Am. Soc. Rev.	Acta
7	Theory construction	+	+	+	+	1.19	1.14	1.15	1.36
8	Hypothesis construction	+	+	+	+	1.10	1.21	1.15	1.36
9	Model construction	+	+	+	+	1.10	1.21	1.11	1.24
10	Variable construction	+	+	+	+	1.19	1.29	1.11	1.12
11	Usefulness to society	−	+	−	−	(2.52)	2.11	(2.22)	(1.52)
13	School's usefulness	+	−	0	0	1.90	(2.04)	—	—
15	Mathematical model	+	+	+	0	1.81	1.61	1.05	1.00
19	Analysis method	−	+	−	−	(2.38)	2.82	(2.40)	(2.08)
26	Language	+	−	−	−	3.38	(1.18)	—	—
27	Number of pages	−	−	+	+	(6.48)	(4.96)	2.18	1.76
28	Researcher's title	−	−	+	+	—	—	3.15	2.88
29	Disguise of defects	+	−	+	+	2.67	(1.86)	1.20	1.04

and Table 17 just shows the tendencies as perhaps not quite so strong as we could have expected.

There is a general tendency for lower means going from the Ph.D. sample to the *Acta* articles, but this does not hold for the first four values (7–10), which instead reflect the relatively high proportion of theoretical articles in *Acta Sociologica,* securing this sample the highest mean for three of the four construction values.

We might still try to see, if we can find in the theoretical cluster the same relationships we found in the empirical one between the mean of a value grade in a sample and its criterion importance. But then we evidently must not use the scientific values we have already used in analysing the empirical cluster once more. They must be excluded, which leaves us only nine values (actually only eight or seven in each sample). But let us try. The remaining values are given in Table 18.

Please observe that in this cluster, exclusion should *not* bring with it

Table 18. *Presence, means of grades, criterion importances and interaction weights in the theoretical cluster of our four samples*

No. Value	Presence in sample				Mean of grade in sample				Criterion importance				Interaction weights			
	Ph.D.	M.A.	Am. Soc. Rev.	Acta	Ph.D.	M.A.	Am. Soc. Rev.	Acta	Ph.D.	M.A.	Am. Soc. Rev.	Acta	Ph.D.	M.A.	Am. Soc. Rev.	Acta
7 Theory construction	+	+	+	+	1.19[3]	1.14[4]	1.15[1]	1.36[1]	−1.00[3]	−1.00[1]	−.04[1]	−.40[1]	1.00[3]	1.00[4]	.42[1]	.85[1]
8 Hypothesis construction	+	+	+	+	1.10[4]	1.21[1]	1.15[3]	1.36[1]	−1.00[4]	−.18[1]	−.04[3]	−.40[1]	1.00[4]	.22[1]	.42[3]	.85[1]
9 Model construction	+	+	+	+	1.10[4]	1.21[1]	1.11[3]	1.24[1]	−1.00[4]	−.18[1]	−.04[3]	−.40[1]	1.00[4]	.22[1]	.42[3]	.85[1]
10 Variable construction	+	+	+	+	1.19[4]	1.29[1]	1.11[4]	1.12[1]	−1.00[4]	−.18[1]	−1.00[4]	.19[1]	1.00[4]	.22[1]	.90[4]	.76[1]
13 School's usefulness	+	−	0	0	1.90[4]	2.04[1]	—	—	.26[4]	.08[1]	—	—	.15[4]	.16[1]	—	—
26 Language	+	−	0	0	3.38[3]	1.18[2]	—	—	.65[3]	.18[2]	—	—	−.12[3]	.49[2]	—	—
27 Number of pages	−	−	+	+	6.48[2]	4.96[2]	2.18[3]	1.76[3]	−.26[2]	−.15[2]	.02[3]	−.01[3]	.15[2]	−.03[2]	.11[3]	.07[3]
28 Title of researcher	0	0	+	+	—	—	3.15[3]	2.88[3]	—	—	.10[3]	.18[3]	—	—	.07[3]	.20[3]
29 Disguise of defects	+	−	+	+	2.67[3]	1.86[2]	1.20[3]	1.04[3]	−.07[3]	−.34[2]	.28[3]	−.10[3]	.25[3]	−.12[2]	.26[3]	.52[3]

[1] The mean is higher than the preceding mean and so we expect more importance too.
[2] The value is excluded from the theoretical cluster, which probably means that it's importance does not change.
[3] The mean is—as we expect—lower than the preceding and higher than the following. Then we also expect medium importance.
[4] The mean is lower than the following and so we expect lower importance too.

Table 19. *Data on the criterion importance of the theoretical cluster for the four samples*

	Ph.D. Importance		M.A. Importance		Am. Soc. Rev. Importance		Acta Importance		Sum Importance			
	$<$ −1.00	$>$ −1.00	$<$ .18	$>$ 0.17	$<$ 0	$>$ 0	$<$ −.05	$>$ −.05	$<$	$>$	$<$	$>$
1. We expect an increased importance				4	1	3		1	3	6	3	6
2. Cluster changed, unchanged importance		1	1	2					1	3	⎫	
3. We expect importance unchanged	1	2			4	1	1	2	6	5	⎬ 7	8
4. We expect a decreased importance	3	1	1		1				5	1	5	1

$<$ indicates values below the median
$>$ indicates values above the median

lower importance, as in the empirical cluster (which dominates the grade sum) but rather unchanged importance, as all non-empirical clusters are equal from this point of view. The data can be seen in Table 19.

The total table to the right and three of the four others come out as we expected them.

The grade means and the interaction weights in the theoretical cluster

Our expectations of the interaction weights in the empirical cluster can not be applied or even translated to the theoretical. We have to start fresh from the beginning once more, although we must use the same five categories:

(1) Mean too high, means in the theoretical cluster that the value is able to give more compensation and so should have more weight. Compensation weight should be high.

(2) a. Mean right although criterion importance is high, indicating that

the value is difficult to attain and thus not useful as compensation. Compensation weight should be low.

(2) b. Mean right although importance criterion low, indicating that the value more easily can be attained. Not very profitable but can still be used for compensation. Compensation weight should be high.

(3) Mean too low, which in the theoretical cluster means that it probably has to be compensated, although its ability to compensate is lower. Compensation weight should be high.

(4) Value not present in the theoretical cluster, but probably leaving some positive correlating with theoretical values, resulting in low weights. Compensation weight should be low.

We use the same classifications in this table as in the previous one on the empirical cluster. The results are:

(1) Mean too high. High compensation weights expected. High in 8 cases of 9.

(2) a. Mean right, criterion importance high. Low compensation weights expected. Low in 6 cases of 6.

(2) b. Mean right, criterion importance low. High compensation weights expected. High in 4 cases of 5.

(3) Mean too low. High compensation weights expected. High in 6 cases of 6.

(4) Value not present. Low compensation weights expected. Low in 4 cases of 4.

This is a good result and evidently the validity of the interaction weight can be taken for granted.

Summary

The main points in this chapter are:

(1) Our samples of articles from *American Sociological Review* and from *Acta Sociologica* show clearcut compensation patterns in their matrices of intercorrelations.

(2) The empirical cluster and the theoretical cluster we found in our previous samples of Ph.D. theses and M.A. theses are found in our two samples of articles. There is thus an evident general pattern for the interaction of the scientific values in all our samples.

(3) Researchers from different samples of publications have many scientific values in common, but in several cases they pay decidedly more (or less) attention to a value and use it in other contexts than researchers from other samples.

(4) These deviations of grade means are bound up with changes in the value's cluster.

(5) As the grades' sum is highest in the Ph.D. sample, lower in the M.A. sample, still lower in the articles from the *American Sociological Review* and lowest in articles from *Acta Sociologica,* we expect the grade means for each value to show the same falling trend. We have used this expected trend to point out cases where importance criterion should be high, medium, or low. The data have supported these expectations and so our frame of reference as well as the validity of the criterion importance can be considered secured. (6) We have used a similar technique to point out the cases where interaction weights should be high or low. The data support our expectations and thus the interaction weights can be considered valid.

CHAPTER 8

The Researcher's Role in his Research Group, his Department and his Field

How does the researcher learn his scientific values?

Researchers learn their scientific values from several sources, as undergraduates from their teachers, as graduate students their contacts with professors are more intense and probably more enduring as a result. There may be an additional selective process with graduate departments selecting those students whose scientific values approximate their own.

Research assistants working for stipends may be the most likely candidates to have their scientific values shaped, since they may be eager to accept the scientific values of the researcher they are to assist.

In the selection of a thesis topic, an additional opportunity to acquire scientific values presents itself. In some cases students have little opportunity to choose: a research assistant might be more or less forced to take a part of the project, but generally graduate students can steer their choices of a thesis problem and/or adviser, who will not only help him, but also be a member of his committee, take part in the judging of the thesis at his examination. All this, however, takes place informally, and there will always remain the formal possibility to get another adviser, another problem or to rely more on another member of the committee —or even leave the department in order to go to another department.

This formal freedom to select not only university and department but also problem, theory, method and adviser, freedom even to change all that seems so natural to the American reader, that we must point out, how recently this freedom was established in the United States and how little of it we meet in Europe.

As a contrast, we shall try to describe the recent Central-European university system, still strong in some countries: the student might have a single or only a few universities to choose between; he would choose according to the field he was interested in and according to the stature of the professors in that field. Once he had decided what university he should go to, what degree to work for and which subjects to study, he has to accept his chosen professor's problem field, theory, method and technique and to transfer his set of scientific values as intact as possible to subsequent students with whom he might work. The technique was, or is, simple and efficient: there was just one teacher of the subject, the full professor (he might have an assistant though), whose famous books (famous at least at his university) dominated the reading list and whose official lectures drew all his students—sometimes even students from other fields, compare with Freuds "Vorlesungen für Hörer aller Fakulteten". The student not only had to accept every value, he also had to spit them up again in the dissertation as this was a test of scientific achievement combined with dogmatic faith to the given values—the balance between these two components a bit precarious as this kind of education favored the students unable to make a distinction between faithful acceptance of given values and progress of science. But, of course, once they had got their doctor's degree, they could start research projects that might bring in some new aspects, not too many though, until they had a chair of their own.

This classical European pattern was probably rather usual in the United States too, even after World War I. But the number of students increased, so did the number of universities and departments, although not with the same speed, as the size of departments grew. The depression broke this evolution pattern. Suddenly competent researchers were unable to find a job and had to take, what departments were willing to offer. Once the crisis was over, the evolution pattern came back, departments expanding in all directions, trying to raise as many researchers as possible or to steal them from each other, for instance by promoting them to the rank of full professor, etc. These expanding departments thus no longer could be handled as the leading professor's private little shop. To attract students different specialties must be covered so that a balanced curriculum could be presented. To cover specialities researchers must stand free from the value system of the great old man—or the chairman—of the department. And—as Herman Lantz has shown in a previous chapter—more and more stress was placed on research, less and less rewards given to teaching.

When the educational boom started after the depression, depressed researchers of course jumped at any department job with more pay, higher position or at an university with more status. Thus the mobility pattern was reinforced and as research money came more freely this too intensi-

Table 20. *Factors contributing to the academic evolution*

Factor	Classical European universities	Modern American universities
1. Size of department staff	1 professor, perhaps 1 assistant	Many professors of all kinds
2. Number of research fields covered	One	Many
3. Status system of researchers	Only the full professor has much status	Status according to amount and type of research
4. Mobility of researchers	Limited	Unlimited
5. Difference chairman — full professor	None	Significant
6. Student's freedom of choice	University, department only	University, department, problem, theory, method and adviser
7. Student's independence	Little	Nominally large, practically less

fied the pattern as the grant receiver could use the grant for pressing more out of his department or accepting a better offer from another department anxious to acquire him and his grant. These patterns of large research grants and the general growth of research have been especially noted after World War II in the United States.

The mobility pattern of American men of science after all has some advantages too. Anybody is willing to work at any department, if salary and/or position is good enough. The strong and weak points of universities and departments are well known and openly discussed, in contrast to the European universities, where mobility is low and each department thus is able to maintain the delightful myth of its superiority.

Probably European universities will change in the same direction as the American universities already have, although they will change not only later but also slower and less. The stream of students to the universities is smaller, the balanced curriculum is not even heard of, research is important yes, but the number of disciples is a good measure of the importance of your work, and thus the mobility of the researchers is still rather restricted.

We might try to summarize the main point of our discussion in Table 20 enumerating the factors contributing to this academic evolution or explosion, where the classical European universities could represent one end of the continuum and the United States universities the other.

We thus assume that the first five factors will all tend to give the student more freedom of choice and more independence of their academic adviser or teacher. If we use the summation theory as a frame of reference here too, we would say that all the seven values form a single cluster, that could be seen as counteracting or compensating other values, for instance the security of the individual student, whose future was practically guaranteed by the classical European university once he had matriculated there and found a professor to follow.

We could of course introduce other compensating clusters too, but for the moment we stop here, as we are mainly interested in the problem of how scientific values are transmitted to the young scientists.

The Academic Market Place of Scientific Values

Universities and departments are judged by staff candidates and students according to their bids but also according to their set of scientific values and their ability to handle them. Departments judge candidates according to their chances to accept and attain scientific values. But these scientific values do not fetch the same price on the academic market. Ability to handle statistical and demographic values is paid well in the departments of sociology, while ability to handle social usefulness as it is brought to bear on the fields of social problems or family sociology is paid less well.

We could easily demonstrate these tendencies by studying what fields the new chairs in sociology are dedicated to, although the lack of competent scientists in the fields most in demand might of course restrict these tendencies a bit. And please remember that such a study is simple because it overlooks an important point: what about all those very competent researchers in fields with little demand, who do *not* get chairs.

Another easy and interesting study could be made on the scientific planning values of those projects, that are given grants. He who undertakes such a study must, however, considerably widen his set of planning values, as the set we used in the previous chapters was not only small but also meant for another purpose: to demonstrate the interaction between values.

But this chapter is devoted to the problem how scientific values are transmitted, *not* to the problems of the academic market place, however interesting our own variety of *Vanity Fair* might seem to us. Well, but the courses noted for the scientific values on the academic stock exchange certainly will affect their transmittance. The values important for obtaining a grant of course bring opportunities for hiring research assistants, who then probably will go in for this particular field with these particular values. The scientific values important for getting a chair in the same way attract ambitious researchers anxious for promotion.

We can lengthen this list: values such as computer know-how shorten the time for a Ph.D. or raise its mark, thus attracting some types of Ph.D. candidates; scientific values given priority by the influential sociological journals of course attract the hopeful authors, etc.

Many factors thus exert a subtle pressure on the research candidates to accept certain values and to abstain from others—for these very reasons they are excluded from the set of values we have previously proposed. Scientists of the Veblen-type probably would not want a grant but hardly receive it if they wanted it; they would find it hard to obtain a chair and very difficult to transfer their scientific values to young researchers eager for a high mark on their theses, a quick promotion and good chances for publication.

Sociology all the same has many lone wolves, how is that possible then? Well, classification of lone wolves is outside our scope, but let us point out two different kinds all the same: the scientist, once interested in his special field and then too fascinated to leave it and his contrast, the temporary worker, who believes that this field soon will be fashionable; the one infatuated, the other speculating on rising values.

We have tried to show how the importance of the scientific values could be measured not only as their power to produce high marks on dissertations (which we already have discussed), but also as their grant producing power, their chair producing power or their publication power. We then assume that the young graduate student in the academic market place adjusts his pick of scientific values to their producing power, as it is demonstrated by the market itself. Powerful sets of values thus not only give more power but also more graduate students accepting them; and the isolated researcher's unique set of values is accepted by nobody, thus keeping him a lone wolf in his cage.

But then of course we have that peculiar phenomenon *fashion* or whatever it is called. Suddenly a field, with little active research for many years, is filled with eager prospectors, staking their claims all over the place and often striking some kind of stuff they believe to be gold. But it seems to be remarkably difficult to predict in advance which field will suddenly bloom this way. There are after all so many unopened and so many half forgotten fields, worked just by a few scientists, that a long-term prediction for an invasion of researchers, moved by rumors and a rising course on the academic market, is difficult or hopeless.

84

The sudden invasion of new fields is of course accompanied by the slow or rapid evacuation of the old ones, which at least can be predicted in principle, although not in detail. A respected field can for instance suddenly be considered controversial.

In general it may be stated that research will develop around fields that are encouraged by strong support. Even here there are exceptions, for example, in the United States there has been a considerable amount of federal and state support for the sociology of the aging. Nevertheless, there have been few takers; and the field has never really developed. A similar forecast might be made for the sociology of dying; a field which has recently attracted some interest. It may be that these kinds of fields represent special areas that will never develop, regardless of the amount of financial support available.

We have tried to apply the theory of the academic market to the problem of how researchers select their scientific values. Before leaving this problem we could also try the summation theory and see what further aspects it might give.

We start with a sample of graduate students, not yet quite sure of the department, the field and set of scientific values they are to choose. Let us assume we can pick their decisions and register each set of values as a preference for a number of values. We then compute the correlations between the preference scores for each value and enter the results in a matrix. We expect every important set of values or important groups of similar sets to come up in the matrix as a cluster of value preferences, having positive correlations with the values in the same cluster and negative to those in other clusters.

This expectation is unrealistic. There should in practice be little chance that the common sets of values would have so little in common and little chance to include the less common scientific values in our list. That would rather make us expect a matrix demonstrating a unified value pattern of only positive correlations, where the most preferred values could be pointed out as a kind of corevariables, highly correlated with each other.

But then such a matrix would demonstrate that although the rare value sets of course should be included in the matrix, these values would not carry much importance to outsiders and only give a small compensation for the loss of the dominating values.

Well, we need not look at it that way. Please remember that the dominating scientific values dominate because they dominate the academic market-place, put pressure on people to move into highly competitive areas, where the method must be first class, the theory highly polished and the latest references taken care of. Those who dislike the role of the White rabbit in the Wonderland of social science, who resent stress, who (like Eeyore) characterize new-fangled methods as "modern behind the ears nonsense" and who stick to their dear old theory, those certainly get a lot of compensation from a set of values that we somehow have lost in our own list. There is for instance the chance to show character, independence and perseverance in never giving up a problem nobody else is interested in. There is the chance to shrug your shoulders at critique, unsympathetic letters from editors of scientific journals or disapprovals from foundation administrators. They are ignorant, stupid and besides malevolent. And that is true in some cases.

What about the researchers who go into a barren field to work there for some time? Well they generally do so because they see an easy chance to apply a new method that they know how to handle or use a new theory that they have to try. The field might be considered little rewarding, but these workers probably get more than compensation for their efforts—and besides have a ticket in the scientific lottery that might win them a prize.

Introduction of the Empire Builder

Why should a research field be evacuated? Well, the easy answer is that the important problems are solved, the rewarding problems picked out and so only the less important or less rewarding are left in this particular field to remain there. This is, however, unlikely. Important problems generally give raise to new and just as important problems. If a problem is rewarding or not depends on changes in method and theory, so a set of not rewarding problems will in a short time contain several ones, which have become ripe and rewarding because there are now new methods to tackle them and/or new theories giving them priority.

Our discussion in the previous sections does not give us any clues. It just said that nothing succeeds like success. Once a set of scientific values has won importance, this set gives priority not only for good dissertation marks but also for grants, promotion and publication. This might give still more grants, promotion and publication, but generally the trend is soon broken. The simplest explanation is of course the balancing effects of the academic market: many scientists are attracted

86

to the important sets of value and the access lowers the demand, at the same time reducing the importance of the important set.

We admit there is something in that explanation, but we do not believe that other explanations should be excluded. Some fields have such difficult values to handle that only small numbers of scientists are drawn into them, and yet they can lose their importance although the access of researchers in the field still is very restricted.

Let us have a look at a rapidly invaded field. Its set of scientific values is not definite yet. The most prominent researchers of our field differ somewhat from one another but those who achieve the top ranks, who first get the choice, the large grants with the influential publications, also attract most attention and many graduate students. They know this very well, use each hard earned victory to secure success: the well received publication is used for obtaining a vast grant, that makes it possible to retain a large staff of qualified researchers, give them offices, equipment and many graduate students to take care of. But this background can be used for many purposes.

First our famous researcher can expand his personal empire by using its resources to get better terms from his chairman, his dean and/or his president. He is valuable for the department and thus should receive an appropriate position, a high salary and various other benefits. Otherwise he might go to another department able to appreciate his services better or at least to pay more for them.

His second expansion direction could be his scientific association, getting on as committee member, editor of its journal or in the end elected president. Of course, the fact that he has trained many of the members will help him, as they expect him to remember them and help them back.

His third approach might aim at the scientific foundations, the research councils or the government agencies interested in his field. He needs them for grants, yes, but he can at the same time show himself useful in his contacts with them, give advice voicing the correct opinion, learn their jargon and respect, or pretend to respect, their bureaucratic technique. Then of course he would be more useful—and have a better chance for further grants.

The empire builder thus uses all his contacts as resources for mobilizing more resources. But of course he soon clashes with the other empire builders, colleagues or administrators from the university, the association, the foundation, the research council or the government agency? No, that is not the pattern of the modern empire builder. Certainly each one of these personal empires has a rise, a decline and a fall (or fading out), but they try to avoid the devastating feuds with their neighbors; they prefer to cooperate.

Let us review the technique a successful researcher and empire builder could use for expanding in the three directions we have discussed. He would see the chairman as another empire builder, trying to make the most of the department. So our researcher would point out how the chairman could attract more students, resources, and grants to the department by allocating more resources to this new empire inside it. And in the same way a successful department would constitute not only another empire but also an important part of the dean's personal empire on the next level, and so on. No need for conflicts here, as long as the resources are sufficient. And even inside a department two competing empire builders try to avoid the competition pattern and sometimes succeed to cooperate on this minor project.

The association of course is the place for cooperation and adjustment too, or—if you prefer to look at it that way—for exchange of rewards. I will support you next year if you support me now, etc. Groups will be formed, broken up and reformed according to circumstances, but every empire builder will try hard not to offend anybody and not to commit himself so far to anybody that he cannot join another important group. The atmosphere has a peculiar blend of overt friendliness and latent suspicion, as it is difficult to draw a line between cooperation and exploitation—and trying to exploit others, you suspect them to exploit you. And so we are back to the academic market place where you exchange support and risk to be cheated, as support is a very perishable ware.

The foundation is after all also an empire or a system. The foundation representatives are recruited from the researchers, but that is not the point here, the point is that in the academic market place they are exchanging grants for material useful to build up their own empire. They want project reports proving their eagle eye for hidden qualities in applications; they want projects useful to society—in this case identical with mass media, mainly the press. And so they stack their money—or rather the foundation's—on sure winners in the top rank but also make some smaller investments in hopeful and grateful youngsters, who then will be anxious to pay back in other currency. Foundation administrators thus tour the country for talents, but probably looking more for ideas and projects useful for their ordinary crew than for new recruits.

Yes, but if nobody round the empire builder interferes with his building mania; a lot of important people even supporting him by using him as a part of their own empire, then scientific empires could go on growing in all directions like a mushroom—and we know that very few do. There must be a brake built in somewhere. Well, probably several, but we are in this chapter discussing the transmittance of scientific values from professors to graduate students and we thus turn now to the relation between the empire builder and the subjects in his empire, his disciples. How does empire building affect the scientific values of the builder? What are the consequences on recruitment and value sets of the disciples?

Well, the empire certainly must have its foundation in research, that is in a set of scientific values, and a good set too, to attract favorable reviews, grants, graduate students, etc. But the empire builder then has to give more time, more resources, more energy to his role of empire builder and not only less of all this to his role of researcher but also less weight to all the scientific values included in his own set.

He probably takes on more projects and a larger staff, although he has less time for them and his set of scientific values loses attraction when he openly pays more attention to his administrative values than to his scientific. When all money from a grant is spent, the researcher must terminate his work even if that means serious loss of data and a bad report; when results point in a dangerous direction, they are toned down a bit; the recruitment of good researchers is no longer as important as the recruitment of good empire builders, willing to take on responsibility for a project and to run it, although often not competent to do so.

We believe that if a field becomes attractive to empire builders, and they are able to dominate, their scientific values become less important to them and the results that emerge may be affected.

What about the empire builder if he is caught in an unfavorable situation? Well, he still has his contacts, his experience, his record and his good reputation. He can use them in many directions: move into another scientific field, take over the chairmanship of a department or even try his arm as a dean; he can accept a job at a foundation or at a government agency, etc. We need not care for him; he is extremely competent to take care of himself. He belongs to the establishment in every sense of the word—and the establishment belongs to him.

But he has lost his chance to transmit his special set of scientific values to graduate students, when he himself no longer takes this set of his seriously, and trades it for non-scientific values. This trade is another aspect of the academic market place, where many things can be sold and nearly everything bought.

Our next point is how to secure empirical data on transmittance of scientific values from professor to researcher recruits and data on the career patterns of empire builders. We admit from the start that we do not know how to study transmittance of values, unless the situation is extraordinary well adapted for such a study.

Still, the problem of value transmittance is important, and if we show how it can be done in the classical European departments, maybe someone else can solve the far more difficult and far more important problem of how to measure the transfer process in the mobile, American departments with their balanced curriculum, their large faculty and their freedom of choice.

A Technique To Measure Value Transmittance From Professors to Readers

We can do the type of study we propose here only on researchers who have published at least three books or articles and who have all been together in the same department for a long time. We are then restricted to the classical European departments, each with a single full professor and a set of qualified readers (docents). We could take for each of these researchers his three last important contributions and grade each publication on all the scales we have suggested and placed in the appendix. We could thus construct a scientific value profile for each publication. These profiles could be used for comparing:

(1) For each researcher his first, his second and his third publication. The greater similarity between the author's publications, the greater *value rigidity* we attribute to him.

(2) Similarity between the professor's profile and that of each reader. We call this just *value similarity* between professor and reader.

We should thus be able to study the effect of different factors on scientific value similarity, interpret this similarity as a result of value transfer. We expect for instance that high rigidity will be associated with strong similarity. We shall return to this technique in the next chapter, where we might get more out of it.

Can we study the career pattern of the scientific empire builder?

We must start from a given population and given data. Let us make our task as concrete as possible by selecting *American Men of Science. The*

90

Social and Behavioral Sciences (Tempe, Arizona: Cattell, 1962, 1968) as our source book. We could take a sample of sociologists there and for each one in the sample register a number of variables, background variables as well as appointments, publications, honorary posts, government assignments, etc. The more common an attribute is, the less value should it possess. Thus everyone would be born, nearly everyone a Ph.D., but already the full professors are a minority. If we avoid pitfalls, we should be able to construct a series of attribute combinations from the common starting point up to the top position with just a few attribute holders. We could assume that all empire builders do or have to follow the same pattern, which would make our combinations a Guttman scale, the prediction power of which could be tested with the usual reproduction coefficient. Probably this assumption is too bold. There might be a common starting point, but still different ways of collecting enough points for the next step on the ladder. If so, this could be analysed with our dear summation theory, as it means that one value or cluster of values might compensate another. We should thus compute all the correlations between all our empire building variables, put them in a matrix and look for clusters. If no clusters turn up, that is a unified value pattern, which could mean either that there are no alternative ways—or that we have chosen a sample where the top positions have all top attributes, the middle positions a medium portion of them and the bottom positions few of them (thus the positive interclass correlations hiding the negative intraclass correlations).

This last point is a bit disturbing because we *have* taken a sample from the top to the bottom and so we *should* expect a unified value pattern, may be even an acceptable Guttman scale. All right, he who really wants a Guttman scale of empire building attributes stands a good chance to get it this way. He who is looking for alternative empire constructions, some of them rare but yet able to compensate for the standard attribute combination, should take another kind of sample: either only the top (which would be relatively easy) or only the level just below the top (which would be difficult).

We are all the same not quite sure, what "the top group" does mean in practice. We could *not* use the attribute combination in the inner-most circle, because that would exclude from the start all alternatives to that special combination. Positions like chairman, dean, etc. would not do, as many famous empire builders avoid that type of administrative positions. But if we start looking for full professors having three publications and at least two of them books or articles in top journals and having held top honorary positions in the American Sociological Association, it is just as bad, because then we lose our chance to study the effect of these attributes in the career pattern. Everyone will have them. We do not want to lose variables that might give important information, just because we have to use important variables to pick out the elite of the sociologists.

One way out of this dilemma is to use some other biographical directory, such as *Who's Who in America* (Chicago, Illinois: Marquis, 1966), where sociologists would have to compete with all other kinds of celebrities and thus so much reduced in number, that we might call them the top in terms of directories.

Using two directories instead of one gives us some more information of background variables, but the main point is that we have got rid of the duty to define how they select names for *Who's Who in America*. (See its foreword.) There is thus a decided risk that this sample might tell us how to be included in *Who's Who*, instead of unveiling the alternative patterns of empire building.

If we still go on to see how this sample from *Who's Who* can be used we could obtain information on the following aspects of empire building:

(1) *Academic Performance*
    1. B.A., B.S., etc.
    2. M.A.
    3. Ph.D.
    4. Honorary doctor.
(2) *Academic Positions*
    5. Instructor.
    6. Assistant professor.
    7. Associate professor.
    8. Full professor.
    9. Research professor.
    10. Chairman.
    11. Vice dean.
    12. Dean.
    13. Vice President.
    14. President.
(3) *Honorary Posts in Association*
    15. Officer, for example, of a regional sociological association.
    16. Officer, American Sociological Association.
(4) *Interaction with Foundations*
    17. Grant from them mentioned.

18. Assignment from them mentioned.
19. Position in them mentioned.
(5) *Interaction with Scientific Councils*
20. Grant from them mentioned.
21. Assignment from them mentioned.
22. Position in them mentioned.
(6) *Positions or Assignments from State or Federal Government Agencies*
23. Grant from them mentioned.
24. Assignment from them mentioned.
25. Position mentioned.
(7) *Military Assignment*
26. Military rank from ensign upward.
(8) *Publications* (better studied in *Who's Who* than in *American Men of Science,* where not more than three publications are cited)
27. Number of publications in *Who's Who*.
28. Number of articles in top journals given in *American Men of Science,* (max. 3).

These 28 variables can be handled in two different ways:

(a) They are considered as present or not present. The more seldom an attribute is present, the more weight it might have (within the limits of common sense).

(b) Empire building is a slow process. We expect the rare and heavy attributes to come late, the common earlier. But this can be checked by looking at the year of promotion, assignment, publication, etc. We had better plan such a check. But we could also use such data to compute correlation between attribute X coming *before* attribute Y, etc., and thus secure the direction in the correlation. We then no longer risk the possibility that Y might have led to X.

We can evidently use our 28 variables in three ways: see them as concentric circles, where you (nearly always) have to be admitted to one before you are accepted in the next.

Or see them as correlated attributes to be studied with a matrix in the hope that compensating clusters turn up.

Or give the correlations a direction and thus making the matrix easier to interpret but probably difficult to handle from other points of view.

There is, however, little sense in planning this investigation in detail now. The researcher undertaking such a study or a similar one will

93

certainly bring his own set of scientific values to bear on the problem. But there is still one aspect of the empire builder that we have not mentioned: his background.

Who's Who in America and American Men of Science do furnish us with valuable information.

29. Name, that could be classified as old stock, Irish, French, Scandinavian, German, Latin, etc.
30. Sex. Empire builders probably completely dominated by men.
31. Year of birth, that is age.
32. Place of birth: Yankee states, Eastern, Midwest, West, South USA, Canada, Europe, etc.
33. Rank of university giving Ph.D. degree.
34. Fraternity, sorority. Number of them mentioned.
35. Marriage, yes or no.
36. Church affiliation.
37. Number of clubs mentioned.
38. Member of a chivalry order or more. Highest degree attained: knight, officer, commander, grand officer or grand cross.

We have taken these attributes or variables because we expect that names having a respectable ring of American background more easily are accepted outside the research sector, that the same holds true for men, youngsters, those born inside U.S. Ph.D. from highly prestigeful universities certainly gives an advantage in the start. There might be a similar effect connected with Greek letters. Marriage ought to be useful for taking and holding those contacts with married superiors so characteristic to American society (from the European point of view). Church affiliation and clubs do give an impression of solemn responsibility that might come in handy to compensate lacking attributes already mentioned. The chivalry orders and Legion of Merit are of course rare in our material, but could be very useful variables for the study of other materials or problems.

This set of ten variables might interact not only with one another but also with the twenty-eight variables given previously to characterize empire building. We thus propose that they are added to this set and analyzed together with them in matrices of the intercorrelations. Thus we should be able to see whether the background might influence choice of alternative empire building programs. Our guess is that background variables are important and that flaws in background not only have to be compensated, but that empire building also might be seen as a kind of grand scale compensation for lacking background. This last idea would suit Adler, but can of course not be tested in our sample, as it is restricted to the top rank.

CHAPTER 9

The Values of the Departments

Departments are organized for teaching and research. They should attract as good students as possible, give them credits and degrees, attract teachers and researchers, give them resources for scientific work, help them to grants and to publications. The department of course can do very little for its faculty in some of these areas, such as publishing, but on the other hand grants, articles and books are relevant all the same, because the department attaches great importance to them. They are values to the department, just as number of students, standard of students, number of degrees, standard of degrees, number of faculty members, their quality, the curriculum, etc.

We have previously discussed a similar approach in chapter 7, when we used the classical European department as a contrast to the modern American department, which we characterized as large, in terms of number of students, of fields covered by specialists, of faculty members and grants, well qualified in terms of many full professors, mobile as students and faculty members are taken over from other universities and will stay only as long as conditions suit them. And then we pointed out that the chairman probably will be kept so busy with administrative problems that he does not interfere with the scientific values of the departments, giving faculty members and students a free hand to choose fields, problems, methods, and other values according to their situation and their interests. But we needed this contrast between the European and the American departments to point out the totally different way scientific values were taken over—in Europe from the only full professor, with a monopoly on his science making his set of scientific values the only possible, and in United States the very complicated Academic market place offering all sorts of scientific values on terms not quite as easy as they first look.

Now we have to look at the value problem from another angle, no longer from that of the researcher, but from that of the department. After all the department also is in the Academic market. How many and how high bids can it afford? How much will they be appreciated? But the department not only has to consider its position in relation to other departments in the same field but also in relation to the other departments in the same university competing for the resources of this university. And we have to look not only for values useful at these levels but also for values or variables which might give us some information about the interaction and change of the department values, considered important in the market. We thus suggest a number of values and try to divide them in groups.

The values of the department, a preliminary list

In order not to mix up the variables with previous sets, we start their number with 51. We try to keep apart values pertaining to teaching, research, and social interaction in the department.

(1) *Values pertaining to teaching in the department*
　51. Number of students taking courses in the department.
　52. The proportion of these students taking a B.A. with a major in sociology.
　53. The proportion of graduate students at the department in relation to 52.
　54. The proportion of these graduate students obtaining M.A. degrees.
　55. The proportion of M.A. students obtaining Ph.D. degrees.
　56. The proportion of Ph.D. from the department obtaining "a good university position".
　57. The number of positions as teaching assistants.
　58. The number of teaching faculty members.
　59. The proportion of highly qualified members of the faculty.
　60. Number of textbooks, etc., published by the faculty of the department during the last five years.
(2) *Values pertaining to research in the department*
　61. Number of research assistants.
　62. Number of researchers at the department with a Ph.D.
　63. Grants given to these researchers during the last five years. Sum.
　64. Grants spent by these researchers last year.
　65. Number of articles in scientific journals published by them during the last five years.

66. Number of monographs or reports in book form published by them during the last five years.
67. Number of research assignments from government agencies, etc. to them during the last five years.

(3) *Values pertaining to the interaction in the department and with the university office*

68. The social climate of the department. We discuss this variable later on in detail, but have to admit that we see no easy method to measure it—at least not in American departments.
69. The rank of the department in the field.
70. The rank of the department within the university, measured by the part it receives out of the allocation of university resources.

We could use this set of department variables to study some interrelated problems of the Academic market place:

(a) How have the American departments of sociology changed in these respects? The educational boom of course has multiplied the number of departments, made most of them larger and more research centered, etc. Such a study might show the expansion pattern, but we predict that even a careful analysis of all the variables' intercorrelations in a matrix probably only will show that the rapidly expanding departments expand rapidly in all directions and that slow or stagnant departments are slow or stagnant in nearly all directions. That is, if we select a sample of sociology departments, register their changes in grades on these 20 department value scales, compute their intercorrelations and enter them in a matrix, we would get nearly exclusively positive correlations, that is a unified value pattern.

(b) Are there then no different strategies in the market that could be identified as competing or compensating clusters of variables? If so, they cannot be pointed out, unless we use another type of sample, taking only departments that started at roughly the same level of resources for instance in 1950 and ended up at roughly the same but much higher level in 1965. They have then had the same increase of resources, but they might have used them in somewhat different ways, allocating more resources to teaching or more to research and qualified scholarship. Their research interests could also diverge, stressing for instance problems useful for society, grants and assignments from official authorities (probably using hard data techniques) or they could stress theory, methodology for the sake of its own, and high class publications, that is in the top journals. If so, the intercorrelations between the changes in grades on

98

our scales ought to indicate compensating or competing clusters in the matrix, that is a compensation pattern.

(c) We could restrict our sample to a number of not too dissimilar departments at a sample of universities now, register their grades on our 20 value scales and compute their intercorrelations. The matrix should then show only positive correlations, that is, a unified value pattern, as the large departments would be able to secure high grades for really all values and the small ones generally would have to be satisfied with low grades. The statistician would say that the positive interclass correlations dominated the intraclass correlations.

(d) We might focus our interest on differences between departments in social anthropology versus sociology, social psychology and as the top subject in this case, psychology. These four departments all belong to the behavioral sciences, but differ in approach and methodological sophistication, which seems to mean that psychology has more status than social psychology, etc. If so this can be handled as the 21st value and should show interesting associations with the previous 20.

We admit that these four projects do not look too tempting. Maybe we could make them a little more interesting by suggesting an appetizing hypothesis. Maybe the field would also be made more attractive if we could point out variables more relevant for the interaction in the departments. And at last we should also try to get some overall impression: is there any use to try summation theory and value compensation in this field. Well we take the first problem first.

A hypothesis on the interaction of the departments' values

We try to compare three different groups of departments, owing to how useful a major or a degree in the subject would be in the labor market. We thus get attractive departments, moderately attractive, and less attractive ones—from this particular point of view.

The respected departments (statistics could be an example, it is in Sweden) of course attract rather many students taking introductory courses and even some trying a major, but on the whole most students would be eager to use their acquired merits in the market and thus quit leaving a moderate but well qualified proportion to go on, and this proportion reduced for each further step, as they are tempted by the offers in the market to give up their academic career. This selfselection results in a comparatively large and good research staff. We should thus find a cluster of positively correlated department values, containing a large proportion of students taking a major (52), of graduate students (53), obtaining their M.A. (54) and Ph.D. (55), a high proportion of Ph.D.'s obtaining good university positions (56), high numbers of positions as teaching assistants (57), of teaching faculty members (58), of research assistants (61), of grants received (63) and spent (64), comparatively many assignments from government agencies and eventually very good resources allocated to the department by the university.

The less respected departments on the other hand would of course try to attract many students, but probably with a less serious interest in the subject. Thus a lower proportion of them would go on to higher studies (value 51), but once having received their degree, they would all have the same small chances to obtain good jobs, in the labor market, have to stay at universities, although their chances for grants and good positions would be small. The proportion of highly qualified members of the faculty would be small, and the same would hold for the number of researchers with a Ph.D. Probably the department would be allocated a small share of the university's resources. This would give us a cluster containing only values 51 and 58. These values should be negatively correlated with the value variables in the first cluster. We thus suggest that "teaching" is a compensation for research.

To this hypothesis could be added the point that the complicated mechanisms of the Academic market place might be able to adjust the market to small changes in demand or supply of scientists and scientific values, but if the total market, where the academic one only is a small part, changes its demands rapidly, the academic market is disturbed. It takes time for it to get rid of a surplus of competent scientists—should they not be needed—which is unlikely for the present. In the same way a strong demand for scientists in a field is difficult to satisfy, as a large part of those best needed for training graduates, would be bought off and the lack of teachers, etc., thus still more stressed, etc. The economists recognize this type of vicious circle discussion only too well. It might apply to the Academic market place.

We can study department values with attitude scales, but prefer other methods if possible. We discussed in the previous chapter a technique to measure transfer of scientific values in European departments from the professor to the readers, using their three last scientific publications, to compute the scientific value profile of each publication. We could then use these value profiles to compute:

(1) The *rigidity* of value profiles for each researcher by comparing the first publication with the second, and the second with the third.

(2) The *transfer* of values from the professor to the readers by comparing the mean value profile of the professors with the mean value profile for each reader and taking a mean of these individual transfers (maybe some kind of correlation quotient could be used).

(3) The *similarity* of value profiles among the readers. By comparing their mean value profiles with another and taking a mean the same way as in 2.

These three sets of value profile data could be used as a measure of the scientific social climate in the department as a very strong transfer of values (no. 2 above) would indicate an autocratic climate, where readers do take over the values of their professor to a large extent.

Yes, but how are we to know whether the transfer correlation should be considered high, medium or low? Well we could use the rigidity coefficients and the similarity coefficients for the readers to give us reference points on our scale.

Each reader certainly has his own set of scientific values, the consistency of which is shown by his rigidity coefficient. If we take the mean of these coefficients for all the readers, it shows how much attention they give their own values. If they should pay nearly as much attention to the values of the professor, that indicates an *autocratic* climate—and, should they pay more attention to the professor's values than to their own, terms like tyranny or toadyism might be used. Towards the other end of the scale we have the similarity coefficient, showing how much attention readers give each others' values. If they do not heed the professor's values much more than each others' the professor should not mean more to them either, and we could thus say that this department seems to have a *democratic* climate. And should the readers pay less attention to the professor than to each other, we could use the term *laissez-faire* climate.

We have to admit that this scale cannot be used in American departments, and that we have not been able to find a substitute scale.

Few good American departments could, however, today thrive in an autocratic climate. Good researchers would quickly disappear and if the autocrat tried to rule a set of less qualified faculty members, the students would not go to that department. Well, if this really holds true, we could try to use the mobility of the faculty as an indirect measure of climate. Of course, the location of the campus, the salary politics of the university, and the general situation on the Academic market would also influence the mobility. Still, we could try this measure. It could at least be used to compare different departments at the same campus, and maybe, refined and made less sensitive to disturbing factors of different kinds.

How would a tendency toward an autocratic climate affect departments? From our point of view the researcher has to adjust his set of values to his problem and his materials. If he can not do so, he loses opportunities and information. An autocratic climate means that he is restricted in his choice of values, finds it difficult to skip values held important by the autocrat but of little use for the project concerned. And worse—the researcher is not encouraged to bring in values given little weight by the autocrat of his department even if these new values would be adequate for the project. And thus we expect that a tendency toward autocratic climate would tend to reduce the scientific value totals in research reports, reduce the number of articles published (value 65), number of monographs (value 66), and in the long run also grants (values 63 and 64), number of research assistants (value 61) and number of researchers at the department with a Ph.D. (value 62), eventually the rank of the department in the field.

Observe, however, that these points might have less weight for departments devoted only to teaching or to research institutes of applied science, where results are not published in scientific journals. They are not participating in the Academic market the same way as the usual university departments we have had in mind.

Can the summation theory be of use to study departments?

We have used the summation theory here as a frame of reference for our discussion of the university departments. This of course is all right, but suppose that we collected our set of data from a sample of departments, how much of their variance could we explain, using the summation theory? Well it depends on the sample. We should have the best chances with a sample of departments taken so that they had about the same resources.

We then assume that departments tend to allocate their resources in different ways, that is, give their values different weights, and that the values tend to form clusters as they are allocated resources in the same

102

way. Values in one cluster should of course have negative correlations with the values in other clusters.

This idea might be all right when applied to the research project or report, as the resources of the researcher really are rather restricted and have to be allocated very carefully, according to their weight. But departments have much larger resources, less defined, often hidden or forgotten until a special need has to be filled. We thus suspect that allocation might differentiate values and clusters far better in projects than in departments.

The same idea can be expressed in another way. Methodology courses and research training not only point out the scientific values and impress their importance, etc., the young researcher also is trained in allocating his resources between them, as soon as he really has got started in a serious project. But look at the values of the departments! No courses point them out, no discussions impress their importance, no training is given in how to weigh them. The allocation process should generally be less ably handled, more affected by traditions and random influences in the departments than in the research projects or reports. And this should result in lower positive correlations between the value grades within each cluster and lower negative correlations, maybe even weak positive correlations between grades for values belonging to different clusters. The chance to obtain a matrix with a clearcut compensation pattern would be less.

Then the researcher alone has the responsibility for the allocation of his resources. The allocation process of the department is a very complicated business with many persons from different levels involved; and the chairman has to delegate rather important points to people with a set of department values widely deviating from his own. The value set thus should be less consistent, varying from one section of the department to another. Those advocating teaching values will certainly disagree with those advocating research values, the survey experts will disagree with the soft data men, etc. And this tendency to disintegration of department values would of course also weaken the compensation pattern, when and if we come that far.

We could of course go on and find further evidence pointing in the same direction, difficulties in measuring the variables, etc., but still we would not give up the whole idea without trying it one way or another. And after all, sociologists use to stress the social norms: whether people know it or not, understand it or not, have been trained to it or not, a group always tends to form norms or values regulating important behaviors. The more the opinions and/or values vary within the group, the more pressure is brought to bear on the deviant members (up to a point).

There are many propositions of this type, that we could cite. Sociologists simply try to look at the interaction process this way. Well, then let us assume that there might after all be something in this. Unless of course sociologists deviate from the rest of mankind, as they know this tendency and tend to counteract it. If so, we could avoid the enlightened sociological departments and study the rest of them.

We do not press this tendency to integrate value systems within the groups, that is, the department, too hard. We are quite satisfied, having found at least one mechanism said to strengthen the consensus on values within the department.

CHAPTER 10

Value Conflicts of the Scientist

Behaviors are difficult to systematize. We have tried to use the role concept and study its corresponding behaviors as they pertain to the set of values we have given each role. But of course the same value can belong to many roles and then be important to one role, unimportant to another. This we call value conflicts (role conflicts would also do) and we try to classify them in three different groups:

(1) Conflicts between the scientist's different scientific subroles about scientific values.

(2) Conflicts between the scientist's scientific values and his other academic or intellectual values.

(3) Conflicts between the scientist's scientific values and the values of his background and every day's life.

We admit that these classes of conflicts do overlap. Still, we can use them for the rather simple discussion we are aiming at.

Conflicts between the subroles of the scientist

We have previously dealt with the interaction of scientific values at three different levels: the research work itself, the scientific group working on the same project or on similar projects, and eventually the empire building process. These three levels are not supposed to relate to different groups; they rather represent three different kinds of loyalty: to the own project, to the group and to the own empire, however small. We term these loyalties or sets of values subroles: the subrole of researcher, of group member, and of empire builder.

The subrole of researcher has its whole loyalty attached to his own project, trying to make the most out of it, using the methods, the theory and the other scientific values best suited for it.

The subrole of group member gives its loyalty to the set of values accepted by the group, in this case the scientific values.

The subrole of empire builder is loyal only to the empire itself, trying to build up contacts, collect merits, acquire grants, etc.

These subroles need not clash with each other, and if they do, the scientist need not be aware of it. There is a chance that the researcher has use for the whole value set of his group and that he thinks the project very useful for publication, grants and contacts. But of course conflicts could arise, and we expect all the three possible kinds: between researcher and group member, between researcher and empire builder, and between group member and empire builder.

Let us start with the conflict between researcher and group member. The young researcher generally is willing or even eager to take over the values from the research group he is attached to, or from the group of graduate students he is made a member of. Scientific training always implies group influence of this kind and the student unable to establish this sort of contacts probably has little chance to be trained scientifically. We thus imagine that our young researcher has had the values of his group efficiently rubbed in before he is able to understand what the problem in his project really is like. So he probably starts out with flying colors and the whole value set of his group. But when some of these values show themselves impossible to attain and others give a small yield, he is of course frustrated and his reaction is more or less directed against his group. They probably defend their values and this he cannot stand, as it implies he himself is a failure. Of course they try to help him, to rescue something out of wrecked values, etc., but they are not willing to let him take some values off their list or put in some quite new ones. This is, however, exactly what *his* role as researcher demands of *him* and so the conflict is there.

He can solve this conflict by holding fast to the values of the group, making himself a loyal member and a bad researcher. He can give up the group and go in for another set of values better adapted to his project. And of course, he might have so strong a position in the group that they might accept some of his changes, taking the role conflicts it would mean to themselves. Probably all the small scientific groups change a little all the time, because of these compromises, but this does not make the role conflict between researcher and group member less acute or less common.

The conflict between researcher and empire builder, we have already tried to deal with. To the researcher research is the goal, to the empire builder research is only a means. There is no conflict as long as the empire builder has just one project to handle, as long as his value set is the set best suited as merit, publication subject and basis for the next research project. The conflict arises as soon as he has acquired some territory, collected a staff and received important contacts to satisfy. To pay your staff you need grants, to get grants you need publications (of the relevant kind), to publish you need results, but these results have to be not only consistent with the correct value system, they also have to be processed and written down in the report. These two last points generally imply a conflict with the researcher's role. The researcher will not accept a value system not adequate for his project; the empire builder will, since his contacts (in funds, government agencies, scientific associations and councils, etc.) might be more important to him than making the most of a project by introducing new scientific values, not agreeable to these contacts.

The time limit creates another type of conflict; the grant has this or that size, the staff costs this or that per week. When the grant is spent the staff must start on a new project, regardless of how far the first project actually has come. There are of course, always possibilities to raise some extra money, etc., but the conflict remains: the researcher is used to seeing his project through to the bitter end, using his own time to compensate lack of other resources; the empire builder has to allocate his staff resources on his projects not according to their scientific priority but according to their administrative attributes.

And this is really a conflict; no empire builder gives up scientific values with a light heart, as they all once were good researchers, conscious of scientific values and ambitious to satisfy them. But economic and research-political considerations very often are more important to them all the same.

The well established empire builder seldom runs into a conflict between this role and the role of group member, as he seldom is a group member any longer. But the very junior empire builder of course often has to judge the value of group membership from what it gives him in value set, contacts, merits, etc., and what it prevents him to grasp. If he comes to the conclusion that the group has a less desirable set of values, and/or less useful contacts, etc., he will probably leave the group although not with a light heart, as it means that he has made a bad investment of his loyalty and his altruistic personality.

An analysis of role conflict, using Goode's Theory

Goode has presented a paper: "A Theory of Role Strain", *American Sociological Review*. 1960 (Vol. 25, pp. 483–496). We try to make the role conflict problem more concrete by applying Goode's ideas to the most important of the three types of conflicts we have handled: that between researcher and empire builder.

Role conflicts can be conscious or unconscious. The scientist conscious of his conflict between scientific research values and the administrative values of his empire should have little difficulty in deciding from one case to another how hard the administrative pressure is and how much the scientific grades have to be reduced. Harsh foundation regulations, etc. might increase the administrative pressure, but hardly make the conflict much worse, although less regard would be paid to the scientific values.

The scientist who runs into serious conflict of this kind but shuts his eyes to it, can react in different ways. Goode describes four of them this way, if we apply them to the empire builder.

(1) He compartmentalizes the conflict, isolates it from his other action, ignores it or he does not admit that there is any conflict. If the grant is spent and the project only half through, well he has of course to write a report of what was done, but as the grant only had this size, evidently the project was not meant to cover more than was covered. The scientific values are attained to the degree he had hoped for. This means some easily made rearrangement of memories, etc.

(2) He delegates the responsibility for cutting down scientific values to someone else, giving this proconsul of his empire the formal power to allocate the resources of the project, and probably knowing all the time that the resources are inadequate. The proconsul will be delighted until he has grasped the situation, been forced to work out a plan for a much reduced project and then get the staff on his part of it to accept the reductions. And the empire builder has been spared the conflict.

(3) He slowly skips out of the conflict by giving up one of the subroles, certainly keeps contacts, grants and empire but giving up the role of researcher, just keeping it as a disguise, useful now and then for improving non-research contacts.

The empire builder then is no longer building anything, just trying to keep his empire together and is at the mercy of his research staff. As long as that is good and turning out good publications, he can go on. The risk is of course that they may take over, or rather, use their publications to obtain grants for themselves, making their smaller, dependent provinces independent empires. And so the successful empire ends with one or more new empires.

The empire builder thus cannot give up his role of researcher without risking his research empire, but he still has the chance to exchange it for an empire in another field. He might accept an administrative position as dean, he might go to the staff of a foundation or a government agency, etc.

(4) He expands his role relations, for instance with the university office, to inform them about the real situation: that the departments do not give good staff enough resources, that the university does not get its fair share of grants, publication chances, etc. He might just as well get the opposite idea: researchers are not really aware of what the nation needs; more attention should be paid to applied social science, administrative points of view, the foundations' wishes, etc., as they certainly know what kind of research is best needed.

(5) To these four mechanisms Goode adds a fifth, not really a way to handle role conflicts, but still a mechanism of interest: the mechanism for preventing the growth of the empire out of the allowed size: the more contacts the empire builder acquires, the less time he has for research and report writing. The start is easy to describe: good publications give good grants to hire good researchers to do good research, reported in good publications giving good contacts and high honorary posts. This can go on for a while, but not in the long run. The posts and the contacts take too much energy and resources, create too many obligations for the research work, restrict the set of scientific values and lower the quality of research and reports. Contacts can compensate scientific quality at least for a while, but the expansion curve is quickly broken.

These five points seem to have relevance for the researcher's role conflicts. But the main point is that these types of conflicts are common and more or less impossible to avoid. A good researcher not only has had them, will run into them again but also is able to stand them. He generally can see them clearly, although in his own terms, and that of course is a great help.

There is hardly any possibility to measure these role conflicts unless we try to use attitude scales or possibly decision games: How would you act, if you were in charge of a project under the following circumstances ... etc.

Conflicts between scientific values and other intellectual or academic values

We try to avoid the problem of describing or discussing this type of value conflict by the simple technique to place the scientific values in one role and other intellectual values in the role of citizen, the role of cultivated academician, etc. We might classify that way, but would we act that way too?

Take for instance a scientist with a strong leftist orientation. He is sceptical about what he calls the establishment. Would that attitude just color his role of citizen but not all his role of researcher? When he reads through our list of scientific values, there is a considerable chance that he stops at no. 11. *Usefulness for society,* and starts musing: "the guy who did this list must be rather conservative: useful to society evidently means useful to the establishment. If he had thought the matter over he would have made two different scales, one for usefulness to the establishment and another for usefulness to the oppressed."

Our critical friend could go on and look for values central for his research work and yet not on our list, values like respect for human life, for human thinking, for democracy, for beauty in life, etc.

He considers these values as scientific, as he tries to attain them to some degree in his research, we classify them as values of the citizen, part of the researcher's background of course but still outside the values most important to the scientific value interaction. How do we know? We must admit that we do not know. All we can say is that reading through samples of dissertations, articles, etc., we have not met points there that would give high grades on scales for values such as these. And how do we know that other books, other journals would not give these high grades for beauty in life, etc. Well, we have to admit that if other books and journals do give these high grades, they do so, but we consider them of little interest and of no importance. And how do we know which articles are important? Does not importance depend on the problem? Would these articles, etc., not be of interest for some problems, for instance alternative sets of scientific values to the dominant ones?

Questions like these are not easy to handle, if you want to appear unbiased. Evidently some problems have to be handled very carefully and especially the choice of relevant scientific values might prove difficult. But we knew this from the start, as there are no official sets of scientific values discussed, far less listed.

Only one of the difficult points raised in this section can easily be taken care of: our list of scientific values lacks values like respect for human life, human thinking, beauty in life, etc., because we place such values among the citizen values, not among the scientific ones. But this is not an important point, since we should study the interaction of scientific values together with citizen values and background data. Clusters thus could contain values of any kind and that is all we could ask for.

But the point that scientific values important for special groups of sociologists tend to be excluded by our methods is well taken and deserves attention, when the set of scientific values has to be prepared for a research project in these fields.

Conflicts between the scientist's values and his values in everyday life

We have in a previous chapter discussed the interaction between the scientist's role: researcher, academician, citizen, family man, club and church member, etc. We expected the successful scientist to pay less attention to his other roles than non-scientists do. If we rephrase this hypothesis so that we expect the scientists to pay less attention to a number of values from every day life, this hypothesis could be tested for values such as marriage, church membership, etc.

We should then compare samples of scientists with samples of non-scientists for a number of data. *Who's Who in America* can afford us a convenient source for data on a sample of successful scientists and samples of successful citizens from other fields to be compared with them.

In a previous chapter we have used the same source and a similar technique to indicate how a study of empire builders could be made. Then we planned to study the empire builder's pattern of attributes (degrees, publications, grants, honorary posts, government assignments, etc.) in order to show their importance and sequence. Now we plan something totally different: to compare scientists' adaption to everyday life (as far as *Who's who* can give us data, a serious restriction) in comparison with citizens from other fields.

Which variables can *Who's Who in America* give us and how are we to take out samples? The list of variables would include:

(1) Type of name: American type of name or not.
(2) Year of birth, as age probably has to be kept under control.
(3) Marriage, number of years.

(4) Age at marriage.

(5) Number of children.

(6) Age of oldest child.

(7) Assignments for federal government. Not mentioned – mentioned.

(8) Assignments for the state. Not mentioned – mentioned.

(9) Military commission. No – Yes.

(10) Legion of merit or foreign chivalry order. Not mentioned–mentioned.

(11) Clubs mentioned. No – Yes.

(12) Sons or daughters of the American Revolution mentioned. No – Yes.

(13) Church membership mentioned. No – Yes.

(14) Masonic orders, etc., mentioned. No – Yes.

We expect the scientists to pay less attention to name, to marry later and/or have a lower proportion married at a certain age, if married a smaller number of children and younger children, less assignments, a lower proportion with a military commission, with chivalry orders, with clubs, churches, Masonic orders, etc. mentioned.

What about the sample? Well we could start by choosing at random a sample of scientists, classified as university professors, in age 50–55, and compare it in all these respects with a sample of the same size and in the same age classes from *Who's Who in America,* excluding university professors and scientists in similar positions. Should the results of these comparisons agree with our hypothesis, we might try to make the comparisons in one activity field after another.

We could then take M.D. as one group and compare the university professors with non-scientists (which in this case will probably not give strong differences). We could go on to the Ph.D. group and compare at least four samples: the professors, the university administrators, the educational administrators and those in other types of administrative positions. The D.D. group could give us a comparison between university professors and the doctors that have gone into parochial work. The T.D. group should allow us to compare professors with engineers gone to technical expert jobs or executive positions, etc. We expect the same general type as previously of differences between doctors gone to research and those gone to the labor market at large. But as our samples have the same long training, doctor's degree, this will cut down differences considerably. Maybe no differences are left. If so, that would be most interesting, as it suggests either that the differences between scientists and non-scientists are established already before taking the doctor's degree and/or that the differences are due to interclass differences.

We would then have to go on, trying to study the M.A. level next and so on the B.A. level, to see where the differences begin to show. And if we still did not find any we should start comparing the different samples of academically trained groups with other groups, such as officers trained at West Point or Annapolis, writers without academic background, company presidents or directors without academic background, etc.

Thus we could not only test our hypothesis that research might compensate accomplishments in other roles, but also analyse at least some aspects of the status climbing process in other fields than science. We should then be able to use the same techniques as we discussed for the scientific empire builders. After all, we expect to find varieties of empire buildings in other fields too, business administration, etc.

But the main point for us to test is the partial withdrawal of the scientists from the roles of every day life. If this hypothesis stands the test, it could explain a part of the sociologist's attitude toward every day life: he is less involved in it and thus more willing to look at it with a sceptical eye, making theories about it instead of taking part in it. He finds it quite appropriate to analyse the roles of high administrators, big business men, church-going, etc., and is not only able but also willing to describe the social interaction round these positions or in these institutions giving them a slightly ridiculous accent. And if these guys are not amused but try to hit back they are told they should feel honored by the fact that they have been scientifically studied. So of course they are not very anxious to give ambitious young researchers access to their data or insight in their routine. And if they have to, they prefer to pay the research project and thus secure some influence over its set of values.

Maybe, the researcher is able to fulfill his critical role in society and every day life, considered so important there, not only by himself, because he often is a marginal man, a bit alienated from society and every day life, since he is so engaged in his research. And this to some extent could explain why researchers are so uninterested in making research on the research process. They are enmeshed in it, unwilling to look at it from a distance and certainly not anxious to appear in the slightly ridiculous posture they are less anxious to avoid when portraying occupational groups. It is more pleasant to make a joke than to take it.

CHAPTER 11

The Application of Our Research
Techniques to Other Fields

We have tried to show how the "summation theory" can be applied to the problems of the Academic Marketplace, to the interaction of the researcher's scientific values, to the research groups, to the departments and to the value conflicts or role conflicts of the scientists. One of the scientific values we give a high weight is generalization. Can this theory and/or technique of ours be generalized to other fields? If so, this gives it a higher grade on the scale for generalization value.

What does then "our research technique" imply? Well, we have discussed the academic market place where departments, faculty members, and students select each other, at the same time trying to attain and/or to select scientific values. We have tried to show that the scientific values in research interact with one another: in a representative sample of all kinds of scientific publications we expect all values, or rather their grades, to have positive intercorrelations with each other, but in a more homogenous sample, such as doctors' dissertation, they should form clusters of variables with positive correlations between variables in the same cluster but negative correlations between variables from different clusters.

We thus handle behaviors as indications of values and expect these values to interact in a predictable pattern. A research technique like this evidently could be applied to nearly any field. We choose as our example the family, partly because we have tried to use our technique previously in that field—see G. Boalt, *Family and Marriage*. New York: McKay, 1965—and partly because we have some additional material available.

The Academic Market place compared with the Marriage Market place

We then should study the mutual selection process, no longer of departments selecting members and vice versa, but of men selecting women and women selecting men. This selection process is long and slow, giving considerable weight to coincidences such as meeting at the right time, the right place, etc. In order to make the comparison easier, let us stick to the most important point in the selection process: marriage. Just as we look at the set of faculty members in a sample of departments, we look at a sample of newly wedded couples, evidently having chosen each other.

The married couples selecting each other make it much easier to use the summation theory than departments choosing faculty members, because we can use the same set of values for both men and women, but have to use one set of value variables for the departments, another for the members.

Men as well as women acquire more value on the marriage market if they are young, good looking, have an academic education, receive a high salary, have a good social background, belong to a respected church, live in an upperclass area, etc. Then we can compute for each couple how much the husband is above or below his wife on each grade scale.

But beware. We said above that we can use the same values for husbands as well as women. That might be true, although it does *not* mean that we also can use the same grade scales. Men and women can both be measured with the usual yardstick, still, men are taller than women who should be classified as tall, medium short on another scale than men, even if this might mean that a short man might be taller than a medium woman. Something similar is true about age. Just as men are taller than women, they also tend to be older than their wives. Actually, we are not at all interested in the *real* differences within the couple in age, education, income, etc., we are interested in *estimated* differences. If the young husband is two years older than his wife, he probably is considered as her equal in age all the same; he might need two more years of schooling to be her equal in education and some 50% higher salary to be her equal in that field.

How are we to know what equality in age, years of education, etc. should mean? Well the simplest way would be to look at our sample according to the age difference: which difference class would get most couples in it. If it for instance turned out to be the class with husbands two years older than their wives, it would indicate that this age difference was considered appropriate and thus should be considered as the *equality point*. If the husband is one year older than his bride, he still would be one year too young, etc. And in the same way we could use our sample to ascertain equality points for differences in years of education, salary, etc.

115

There is of course no need to apply this technique to social background, church membership, area of town, etc. Boys and girls still come in the same proportions to all social classes, all religions (with some exceptions) and all areas. There is no need for artificial equality points in these cases.

We could thus register in our sample of couples how great the differences are on each value's grade scale between husband and wife in each couple. The summation theory in this case then predicts that each strong difference for instance in favor of the husband has to be compensated by differences in other values going in the opposite direction.

Why should these correlations be negative? Well, let us construct an example: the girl from the good background with a lot of money and a father with a flourishing business, but still the girl is lacking in charm and in good will too, being too suspicious of boys. She meets a good looking guy, unwilling to take no as an answer and so they are married although he does not have a top education, lacks background and money and will need a lot of support from his father in law, one way or another. Or we have the second classical example: our husband is a Ph.D. and his wife has no more than a couple of years in college. But she is younger than her husband and much prettier, so unless we look at just one variable at the time, we find her equal to him or even a little superior if we just look at her sum of value grades. We are all of us very democratic when it comes to platinum blondes.

We evidently assume, that people are able to pick out a wife or a husband of equal value. But why should they? It would be much more natural to assume that we all try to get something very attractive, far more attractive than we ourselves. O yes, we try. We sigh for the movie stars and top rankers, but they in turn sigh not for us but for producers and top toprankers. When it comes to brass tacks, most of us have to be satisfied with somebody not worth much more than we ourselves. The marriage market is there for just this purpose and does not encourage unwarranted optimism, actually treats is as cheating. So if the difference in value is too large, the more valuable partner keeps an eye on the market all the time to see if something better might turn up. And even if the couple is in love, that is, strangely overrating each other, their parents and friends are not sharing this tendency and extremely helpful in making the most out of any difference in value sum. This way the marriage market can be relied upon to perform its value registration and combination.

We admit that this picture of romance and beauty seeking might seem

116

a little trivial. To select a marriage partner looks like going to a shoe shop and ransack all the boxes, till you find a left foot slipper of the same size, color and trade mark as the right foot slipper you are or wear. But our language has long used these prosaic similes for marriage selection: to match, to make a pair, form a couple, etc. This of course is no proof for our point of view, on the contrary, it should make us a little suspicious that we might be victims of our language habits.

We can not prove that marriage selection results in pairing off couples of approximately equal value on the market. We even admit that other factors might in practice distort our simple model, for instance if one partner is very anxious for marriage he or she might be forced to accept a bid below their course value etc. But if we *assume* equality between the partners, then we can use the summation theory for analyzing how one value might compensate the others, as the outcome of the interaction would be equality in total value sum between husband and wife—or at least a strong tendency in that direction.

The interaction between values in the selection process

The summation theory not only wants us to add the value grades to a sum and use that, it also insists that the interaction between all the values should be studied. We could do that in this case by computing all the intercorrelations between the differences in value grades within the couples in our sample. If we place these correlations in our usual matrix, we would expect the correlations to form a pattern with all correlations positive (a unified value pattern) *or* show some clusters with strong positive correlations between the variables in each cluster but weak correlations between variables from different clusters (compromise pattern, as the positive interclasscorrelations have about the same strength as the negative intraclasscorrelations) *or* eventually show clusters with negative correlations between variables from different clusters (a compensation pattern, dominated by the negative intraclasscorrelations, that we assume to exist).

Let us suppose that we got what we are not expecting, a unified value pattern with only positive correlations. We could take that to mean that our basic assumption is wrong: there are lots of men selecting women far below them in total value sum and at the other end a lot of women accepting men far below them—showing that the marriage market does not work or at least does not work as we thought. Love might be blind or not seek its own. Or—just as bad—people might look for other values in their partners than those we have listed: interaction variables, character qualities, sexual traits etc., variables quite able to compensate a lot of the social values we have made use of. Then we should try to find out and measure such variables, although this might turn out a wild goose chase, since our basic assumption, equality of the partners, could be wrong.

The compromise pattern would not be quite as bad as the unified value pattern. Love would not be quite blind and have some regard for its own, although we might still suspect that we lost some important values and the beautiful compensation pattern they would have brought us.

The compensation pattern is what we expect and hope for. But do we have any real reasons to hope? One cluster would certainly work out since a good social background is correlated not only with upper class living areas and respected churches but also with higher education which tends to give higher salaries. Actually age and looks are the only variables not correlated with that cluster. Looks might be, all the same, as parts of looks come with food habits, wardrobe and even access to look producing cosmetics. These correlations mean that if one in the couple is superior in one of these class-values, he or she probably is superior in all of them—and then how can the inferior partner compensate the whole lot? Well, that's their problem, but we have provided them only with two chances for compensation, which seems stingy. Well, IQ could be used as a third, only it is so obviously correlated with education. Will and ability to fight for the underdog's rights on the marriage market might be another, but cannot be brought into our model of the marriage market, as they oppose the whole idea of that market.

The best matrix we could hope for, thus, would show a cluster of differences in background, church, education and salary that was compensated by looks and youth as another cluster and may be IQ as a third cluster. But it could turn up only if the equality assumption held—and if these values of the marriage market are accepted and given the same weights by all persons concerned. This last point was very difficult to handle when we discussed the scientific values. It is not easier in this field and we might as well give this part of our discussion a sub-heading of its own.

Is there consensus on the values in the marriage market?

Some values of course are accepted by all parts, but some are not. Take for instance the rank of the churches. The sociologist can easily rank them and probably would not give the Catholics even an average rank. But a Catholic would hardly accept that. If strong in faith he would place it first. We can then hardly expect consensus in this case. What consequences does that bring?

Well, a Catholic guy of course can attract and be attracted by a non-Catholic girl. From her point of view his religion would be something he had to compensate, from his point of view his own faith rather would be an advantage. As long as little weight was given this value it would hardly matter, but suppose that the boy found out that the girl's family rated him low because of his faith. He, who really has a religion much superior to theirs! etc. He would probably feel that he needlessly squanders some of his resources in the marriage market to pay for debt that should be a deposit. And then he might react so that he can use his resources to their full value, that is he gives up this girl in order to marry a Catholic girl, appreciating also his faith.

We thus expect that the more important a value is considered and the less consensus it is given on the marriage market, the more frequently people would marry their equals in this respect. Our theory of summation then is of little use and the good old homogamy theory suits the data far better.

What about the heterogamy theory, could that also be easily related to the summation theory? Yes, if we want to. Nearly any theory can be twisted so as to cover, or be said to cover, any other theory. The main point in the heterogamy theory is that people might value not their equals but their opposite numbers. Take for instance a dominant man, he probably prefers a submissive wife, etc. But this need not contradict the summation theory, which says no more than that people try to make as good a choice as possible. Sometimes, as in social class, equality is considered best, sometimes women should have less of the value than men, as age or education, sometimes the opposite number might be the ideal and then this should be recorded as no deviation. Thus the heterogamy theory might be considered as a special case of the summation theory, to be used for values where people consider it important to choose their partner with just as much lack of the value as they themselves have a surplus. The undeniable case is of course sex: all men who marry, marry women.

There is then no basic contradiction between the summation theory on one hand, the homogamy theory and the heterogamy theory on the other. But this result is more or less bound to come, if you want that result.

The Divorce Problem

We expect that couples with husband and wife of equal value on the marriage market should be more stable, run less risk of divorce than the more unequal couples. The more equal, the less risk. But then all these values change with time. The husband generally makes a more rapid career than his wife and this might place her at disadvantage. The housewife completely engaged in children, food problems, clothes, etc., in one sense always is at an disadvantage. Once she was young, pretty, clever, interested in books, her job, the company problems, etc., sharing interests with her husband, but can she share them when she loses contact with them and never has chance to lose contact with kitchen, vacuum cleaner, children problems, etc. She has changed, or rather, has had to change.

Sometimes the man goes down instead of up. He might lose his job or his money, he might start drinking or be sent to prison; he makes himself inferior to his wife all these ways. And we expect that the greater the inferiority and the more suddenly it comes, the greater the risk for divorce.

But we have to admit that the divorce to a high degree depends on how the superior part interprets her or his role in the situation: as a chance to show the true character, as an obligation toward society or as duty toward children and one self to secure another and better adapted partner as soon as possible. Evidently our technique here is inadequate and can cover only a small part of very complicated problems.

The Marriage Market and the Interaction Pattern

We have discussed the similarities between the academic market place and the marriage market. We found it easier to apply the summation theory on the marriage market, since we can look for the same values

120

in husbands and wives (although not the same grade scales) but have to use different scales for the departments and for the faculty members in the academic market place. We are tempted for a moment to try values that could be used on departments as well as faculty members. It could be done, of course, but in our opinion probably little use to come from it.

Now next step is to move from the selection process to the behavior in the family, to its research problems. We register these behaviors as measures in the degree to which values have been attained. Instead of scientific values we now are to list family values and give grade scales to measure them. But in this case we can hardly be expected to give more than a preliminary and rather sketchy list. Something like this:

Values in Family Life

(1) *Ideology pattern of the family*
1. Power structure in the family. Dominance pattern versus equality pattern.
2. Wife's work outside the home. No work – part time – full time.
3. Husband helps with house chores. Not at all or little – to some extent.
4. Family planning. No – Yes.

(2) *The children*
5. Number of children
6. Socialization of children. Autocratic pattern – alternating pattern – childcentered.
7. Educational opportunity given the children: Highschool – junior college, etc.
8. Social adaption of children. Maladjustment – adjustment.

(3) *Style of life*
9. Social class
10. Income
11. Dwelling standard
12. Car Have not–have.

(4) *Cultural standard*
13. Number of books
14. Musical instruments. What kind?

15. Visits to theaters, concerts, museums, happenings.
16. Going abroad for leisure

(5) *Social contacts*

17. Belongs to a church. No – yes. If yes, what church?
18. Belongs to occupational organizations. No – yes.
19. Belongs to clubs. No – yes. If yes, what club or clubs?
20. Belongs to shrines or similar orders. No – yes. If yes, what order?

(6) *Non-cultural standard*

21. Food standard. Below average – above average.
22. Drinking. Above average – below average.
23. Card playing, numbers, etc. Above average – below.
24. Dope addiction. Addiction – no addiction.

We have given all these variables the same direction. What we consider to be lower estimated in society we give a low grade and what we consider highly estimated we give a high grade.

The only really difficult point then is number of children, as now a high number of children seems to be usual among couples with very good economic resources as well as among couples with no resources at all. This makes it difficult to choose direction and so we stick to the simple numerical principle, although we ought to work out some scale of the type: number of children far exceeding resources – exceeding resources – not exceeding resources, trying to use our sample for finding out convenient rules for classifying number of children according to resources.

The interaction of the Family Values

Let us make our usual assumption: we have a sample of families, we register for each family its grade on each of our 24 value grade scales, compute the intercorrelations between 24 grade variables, collect them in a matrix and look for the interaction pattern.

We should find the pattern determined by the sample. If we have used a representative method for taking the sample, we expect the unified value pattern, that is, all correlations should be positive. The top group is able to attain all values mentioned, the bottom group does not attain them and these two extremes dominate every grade scale, thus securing positive correlations.

If we have used a sample with some restriction of range, lacking top group as well as bottom group, we might get a compromise pattern, that is a number of clusters with strong positive correlations between the values belonging to the same cluster but very weak correlations, positive or negative between values belonging to different clusters. (Then the positive interclasscorrelations have approximately the same strength as the negative intraclass correlations, we hope.)

And eventually, if we have taken a sample of families in about the same age and about the same income, we expect a compensation pattern, that is a number of clusters with positive correlations between variables belonging to the same cluster, and negative correlations between variables belonging to different clusters. That would mean that these families with the same frame of resources use them in different directions, one might go in for children and house, education and culture, another might move toward social contacts, higher class distinctions, etc. (empire builders?), a third cluster could use food, car, musical instruments, etc.

It is difficult to predict—and probably just as difficult to interpret— the compensation pattern we expect in the matrix for a sample restricted to a class of families with about the same resources. But it is easy to predict and interpret the unified value system we expect in a representative sample. All these positive correlations could be taken to demonstrate that modern families with an equality ideology between man and wife, allow the wives to work outside the home let the man take over some part of the housework, plan number of children and their arrival, tend to have a child centered atmosphere, give their children higher education and are rewarded with relatively few maladjusted children. This pattern is most pronounced in middle and upper classes, with good incomes, high dwelling standard, cars, number of books, musical instrument, such as piano, or violin, sometimes (not too often) visiting theaters or concerts, etc., and sometimes going abroad in the summer. They tend to belong to (high standard) churches, occupational organizations, clubs, may be a lodge too, they have a well balanced diet and they do not drink above average (?), don't play hazard or use drugs.

This sounds very reassuring to pillars of society, but we must realize, that the clearer the pattern would show in a matrix, the more would it depend on a contrasting group: men who don't care for equality ideology or for helping at home, families who do not care for family planning, nor for the children they have got, for their socialization, education or adjustment. They belong to lower—lower, have small incomes, low dwelling standard, no books, probably no musical instruments, never visit theaters, concerts, etc., never go abroad—how could they—often belong

123

to no church, never to clubs or lodges, have a low food standard but probably drink, play cards or try dope above average. And please—remember that these families may be a small proportion of all families, but that they have many children and thus create difficulties for child guidance clinics, schools and later the penal system out of all proportion to the number of families. Which does not sound reassuring to pillars of society—and is not meant to sound so, either.

A test of the hypothesis

Gunnar Boalt's dissertation (*Skolutbildning och skolresultat,* Stockholm 1947, out of print) gave background and school data for nearly 5000 children in Stockholm, leaving the 4th form in 1936 about 11 years old. This was not a sample but the total population. But a population of children, not of families. Childless families will of course have no chance to be included, families with two children have twice the chance families with only one child, etc.

We intend to use these data from 1947, although they were collected for quite different purposes, in order to illustrate what type of matrix we can expect when we study representative samples.

We can use of the original variables the following 11, selected because they have some bearing on the family background:

(1) Children's grades (credits) total from the primary school fourth form.
(2) The children's continuation to a higher school type in the Autumn term 1936, or later.
(3) The father's or guardian's social class.
(4) The family's income
(5) The family's rent. A crude measure of dwelling standard.
(6) Marriage circumstances. The father married and guardian to the child was the later class; were the circumstances otherwise this was the former class, as it meant some kind of difficulty.
(7) The guardian's age. Not a very important variable, but giving some stability to the family and the income. Younger than average – older.
(8) The child's age. To be older than one's classmates is no advantage and correlated with low IQ. We thus use the direction: Older than mates – not older.
(9) Registered in the files of the social authorities (because of unemployment, etc.), which of course indicates social risks thus: Known – not known.

Table 21. *Matrix of correlations between 11 variables in a population of school children leaving the fourth form of the public schoolsystem of Stockholm in spring 1936*

No.	Variables	1	2	3	4	5	6	7	8	9	10	11
1	School grades	■	+.25	+.32	+.25	+.22	+.14	+.04	+.24	+.35	+.30	+.04
2	Higher school		■	+.71	+.44	+.63	+.18	+.09	+.21	+.58	+.38	±0
3	Social class			■	+.45	+.67	+.21	+.16	+.19	+.50	+.28	−.09
4	Family's income				■	+.51	+.50	+.05	+.17	+.59	+.18	−.02
5	Family's rent					■	+.22	+.14	+.15	+.47	+.21	+.03
6	Father guardian						■	+.01	+.10	+.34	+.12	−.24
7	Guardian's age							■	−.03	+.03	+.02	+.19
8	Child's age								■	+.20	—	+.06
9	Known social authorities									■	+.28	+.14
10	Known law courts										■	—
11	Number of children											■

(10) Registered in the files of the law courts (which means a rather serious crime). These data were collected afterwards by Gösta Dahlström and correlated only with some of our other variables. Known – not known.

(11) Number of children in the family. As the family's number of children is high in upper classes as well as in the lower-lower, the correlations cannot be predicted. We, however, use the direction that would be natural to an American sociologist (not to Swedish) and thus count many children as the low class then going up the scale to one child.

Variables 2, 3, 6, 9, and 10 are dichotomized and all correlations then computed as tetrachoric coefficients. The rest of the correlations are computed as product moment coefficients. We now turn to the correlations between these eleven variables, given as usual in a matrix, Table 21.

We find that the variables 1–10 form a cluster and that variable 11, number of children, as we expected, has some negative correlations. The cluster has 43 positive correlations out of 44 and thus shows a very pronounced unified value pattern. If we include no. 11, we still have 48 positive correlations out of 53. These data support the general picture we have given of the interaction of values. If we use a representative sample and study how a number of values are correlated, they *should* show a unified value pattern of this kind. It is possible thus to apply our frame of reference also to the values of the family.

The family is not only an important but also a universal institution, in need of research, as people seem to have very little knowledge of their own behavior tendencies connected with sex, marriage, and family life. Scientific values are on the contrary well studied, cared for by the most competent group in society, the scientists, and transferred from one generation of them to the next. There should perhaps be less need to study a problem, so competently administered, than to study the scientific problems of the family.

Family Conflicts and Compromises about Values and their Grades

The conflicts between different research groups in the department about their deviant sets of scientific values have several parallels in the family; the most convenient one for our purposes is the conflict between parents and their teenage children.

There are the universal conflicts about the weekly allowance, about the wardrobe, about the time they can stay out on date, evenings, etc., these running conflicts sometimes broken off by compromise, that is called so by the parents, may be not by the children. But even if the teenager loses the discussion about how long he or she can stay out, he or she may not be home at that time all the same. And they generally get away with it, as anxious parents are anxious not to show how anxious they are, autocratic parents may not really care to get out of bed with a watch in hand, since they might look ridiculous instead of imposing, etc. Parents always have weak spots and children always find out, making a difference between the theory agreed upon and the silently accepted practice.

From our point of view the conflicts in cultural values are far more interesting, conflicts about the books to read, the programs on radio or TV, and the records to play on the gramophone. These values deviate so strongly and consistently from parental values that some sociologists talk about a particular teenager culture. We have to admit that teenagers do not accept some of their parents cultural values, but there generally are several varieties of teenager cultures available, quite excluding each other. This is interesting as it evidently would give a very fine compensation pattern if processed into a matrix. But for the moment we are not out to study the interaction pattern, we are out for the conflicts these different sets of values create and the compromises that come out.

Parents often seem to believe that their teenagers pick up their peculiar values and stick to them just to tease their parents. From our point of view that is wrong. Parents then simply do not realize, neither that their own set of values is not universal but anchored in their reference group, nor that their teenagers set of values is dictated by their reference group, the strength of which parents constantly underestimate. And so the conflict certainly is there. What about compromises?

Compromises are possible only if the two groups meet and interact. But generally the teenager is anxious to avoid that, for very obvious reasons, and so no compromises come out. But parents or other adults who are willing and able to respect the value set of a teenager group certainly are able to influence them and probably influenced also at the same time.

The general pattern of the teenagers, however, is to keep their group out of hearing and reach of the parents. The parent's pattern often is an impatient patience waiting for the teenager to give in, change back to *real* values. And in the long run the overwhelming majority do, because their reference group not only changes, it also dissolves or they leave it. Once out of the group, they drop its values, retaining just a few.

This isolation between the teenagers' peer groups and their families on one hand gives the peer group a free hand to form its own set of values; they need not compromise. On the other hand this original and sometimes admirable set of values has a very small chance to survive, because the lack of interaction with adults prevents compromises and any change of the adults.

The scientists then should be grateful for their own ability to discuss sets of values and to influence each other. Our example of the teenagers suggests that if a scientific group isolates itself, it probably will dissolve, leaving few traces.

Conflicts between the individual's various subroles

This problem can be studied on any member of the family: father, mother, teenager, etc. We demonstrate the problem by picking out some convenient subroles:

The father not only is father for his children, he is the bread winner of the household, the husband of his wife, the host for his guests and house owner taking his pride in keeping lawns cut, walls painted or papered, all the small details working.

His wife, of course, has a corresponding set: mother householder, wife, hostess and house co-owner, choosing colors and wallpapers, pointing out furniture to be bought or carried to the attic, taking the daily chore of buying, cooking, dusting. And, don't let us forget the sexual roles, man and wife are lovers too.

Let us stick to the husband's subroles at home: bread winner, father, husband, host, houseowner and lover. The bread winner has to watch the costs of children, family, parties, investments in house and home. Only love should be free from cost considerations, but, of course, it is not, since the emotional aspects of it are so extremely sensitive to all kinds of contacts between the lovers. The bread winner not only has to allocate money resources so as to minimize the conflicts between his different roles, he may also have to raise more resources, by taking over time, etc., in order to pay in cash what he has to withdraw in time and interest. This tendency sometimes is driven so far that practically only the bread winner role is left and the poor guy who has gone in for this solution will probably be a bit surprised, when he finds out the results: the children might not care for him, the family has no place for him, at his parties he may be the guest who has to serve the other guests, the house is no longer his and his wife may have taken a lover. He, who has sacrificed everything for his family! Has he?

The father has to balance the children against his wife, against guests, against the tear, wear and repair of the home and against the wish for privacy, emotional contact and love. The husband role may come in conflict with the parties, etc., etc. We all recognize these types of conflict, and the guilt we feel, not being able to solve them.

The wife's subroles collide in a similar way, often discussed by marriage counselors. The conflicts of the teenagers are less discussed and let us try to apply Goode's categories to them to see what they would look like. We use then only the two most conspicuous roles of the teenager for our demonstration: the role of good son or daughter and the role of peer group member. The conflicts between these two roles are nearly always to some extent open, but hardly ever totally open. Some tensions remain unconscious. So we should look for all the four categories from Goode, which we used in the previous chapter to analyse the scientist's role conflicts:

(1) The teenager compartmentalizes the conflict. He might try to ignore it or maybe not even feel that there is a conflict. His parents are the best people in the world, really doing their best for him. And he has

some wonderful friends too, splendid youngsters who really mean a lot to him. All the superlatives are needed, as they imply that one splendid group cannot be in conflict with another. But, a clinical psychologist might suspect that the superlatives also cover considerable aggression.
(2) The teenager delegates the responsibility, for instance, the daughter to her mother, who does not want her to wear those clothes, visit that place, etc., etc.
(3) The teenager slowly slips out of the conflict by giving up one of the conflicting roles. He might go to college, leave home on some other pretext or give up the peer group. It seems to be a common tendency to give up both the conflicting groups at the same time, which suggests that the conflict went deeply and undermined both the roles.
(4) The teenager expands one of his conflicting roles in order to plead that as an excuse for not attaining to values of the other. He might get interested in a girl from his peer group and have to see her, or he might on the contrary, take over some responsibility at home, and thus be unable to keep the same close contact with the peer group as before.

What may be derived from this illustration?

We think we have shown that it is possible to apply our research technique to another field, that of marriage and family. We have compared the Academic Marketplace with the Marriage Market, the interaction of scientific values with the interaction of marriage values, the transfer of scientific values with the transfer of family values and the scientist's conflict of subroles with the family member's. The discussions here followed the same patterns and the comparisons have in some cases given us a clearer picture of our problems.

Still, this does not mean that the summation theory can be used in every field of sociology. Take for instance schools. Generally, you have to send your children to the school in the area you live in and up to a point you can select that with an eye on the school, but then little more can be done. Your child has to take the teachers he or she is allotted to but has some opportunity to select school type and subjects. Thus, school values apply to school type and subjects and the grade scales for attaining these values are the school grades. One good grade certainly can compensate a low one on the average, etc. The values certainly form clusters, the language cluster, the math-physics cluster, etc. And so there is little left for the summation theory to perform in this field, it has already been used to the uttermost, by ambitious pedagogues.

There are probably other fields where the summation theory is just as useless. But fields that interest sociologists show regularities in behavior and these regularities can be taken to indicate values. Most fields contain many values and man after all has a peculiar drive for rationality and consistency, keeping some order in his values, making a pattern of them, giving up other patterns or willing to do so if he is compensated for it. As soon as values are common, accepted by some consensus, then they can be studied with our technique.

As soon as we use the term use and usefulness, we risk that the reader is taking it as an invitation to ask what the usefulness of our projects for research on the research process would be for the researcher? That is a standing question for every researcher in every field and most researchers have a standard answer. The use would, however, change with subject and problem studied. The study of the interaction between the scientist's different roles as scientist, citizen, family man, etc., might point out to him some risks for conflicts in his everyday life, the study of the interaction between scientific values during the research process might make his decisions and search behaviors more rational. The study of how the scientific values are transferred from one generation of scientists to another might be useful for selection and training of graduates. The interaction between scientific groups could have implications for the organization of research institutions. The study of departments and their values might, sad to say, have a bearing on the allocation problems of the universities, which of course might create trouble. And so at last the study of the scientist's role conflicts between his subroles as researcher, group member and empire builder was meant to give some help to scientists in this situation. But this of course is nonsense. A scientist caught in a severe conflict of this sort is probably little inclined to handle it intellectually. And a scientist in conflict and still able to grasp the analysis of it is sound enough to stand anything, if he stands this.

CHAPTER 12

On Scientific Publications

Our discussions, research and proposed research have generally been based on, or have intended to use, content analysis of scientific publications. We thus should have a look at these: authors, content, publication forms (journal, book, etc.), all of them bound up with country, subject, etc.

Could we use our summation theory? Well, a publication certainly is viewed, by the author at least, as a value and of course scientists look on publications as having more or less value. Let us imagine a greedy sociologist coming to a table filled with sociological books and reprints and being told that he could take ten of them. Which ones would he choose? He probably would look for books from the leading series and publishers, reprints from the top journals, for well-known authors, for high scientific values attained, for thick volumes with many pages, for publications from respected universities, from esteemed fields of learning and recent year of publication. If he could not find ten thick recent volumes fullfilling all his wishes, he would have to let one value compensate another and so we could use the summation theory—at least in that situation.

Scientists up to a point always are in a similar position. What stuff are they to read, to get for their library, to cite and so on. There simply is a publication market, where we should be able to apply the summation theory at least for a discussion. We start this discussion by trying to give scales for some of the most important values involved. Thus, we are not giving attention neither to the book's design, nor to the quality of the editor's work, the book binder's competence, etc. We look at the publication market from the scientist's point of view, not from the publisher's.

Publication Values and Scales to Measure Them

We propose only seven publication values: The reputation of the publication firm, the publication's scientific value sum, total number of pages, the value of the author's name, the university of the author, the scientific field covered by the publication and then eventually the date of publication.

(1) *The reputation of the publication firm.* The large international journals and book-series come out as a top level, the second consists of second rankers, where we might include for instance *Acta Sociologica,* if we try to include European journals too. The third would be little known, local journals, (including those in German or Swedish language) or books from little known presses in the U.S., Europe, etc. The fourth level would include popular scientific journals, series or books.

It would, of course, be easier to make one scale for journals and another for books. But, if we are trying to handle all publications at the same time, we have to use the same scale for articles and books. Besides, number of pages is on the third value and so taken care of as a separate dimension. We thus get the following steps on our scale, from bottom to top:

Grade 1. Popular scientific articles or books.

Grade 2. Local journals (published in English, German, Swedish, etc.) or books in little known series or from little known publishers.

Grade 3. Well-known journals, book series and/or publishers, but not in the top class.

Grade 4. The top journals, book series and/or publishers.

(2) *The publication's scientific value total.* We can use the set of scientific values discussed previously, but should restrict ourselves to a number of the most important ones. Besides, two of the scientific values we have already broken out to use as publication values 3 and 4. We must also get rid of all values which are attributes not of the publication, but of the author. We could keep, for instance, the following set of sixteen scientific values, still keeping their number from the original set of 29:

1. Presentation of hypothesis.
2. Reliability.
3. Validity.
4. Representativity of the sample.
11. The investigation's social usefulness.
12. Problem's news value.
14. Definition of the variables.
15. Mathematical model.
16. Statistical model.

132

17. Treatment of data with scales.
18. Actuality of the scale.
20. Mathematical treatment of the material.
21. Size of the material.
22. Non-response in the material.
23. The fate of the hypotheses.
25. Literature covered.

On the question of scales for these 16 variables see the *Appendix*. We intend here to give the variable 9–10 steps.

(3) *The work's total number of pages.* We count the number of pages in the larger periodicals as double (possibly more if necessary) and use same scale as for variable 27:

1. 10 pages or less.
2. 11–25 pages.
3. 26–30 pages.
4. 51–99 pages.
5. 100–150 pages.
6. 151–250 pages.
7. 251–500 pages.
8. More than 500 pages.

(4) *The value of the author's title (degree).* We make use of the same scale as for variable 28, i.e.:

1. Author neither master nor assistant teacher.
2. Author master, doctor or assistant teacher.
3. Author instructor, research fellow or assistant professor.
4. Associate professor.
5. Full professor.

(5) *The author's seat of learning* we divide up according to how well-known it is to the international readership and/or the publisher. We must be content to suggest a rough division:

1. Seat of learning unfamiliar to the judge.
2. Seat of learning scarcely known to the judge.
3. Well-known seats of learning but not in the top class.
4. Top class seats of learning.

(6) *The essay's academic subject.* Even if different subjects can presumably bear greater or lesser reputation, their internal order of merit

varies from country to country. We refrain from any sort of order here.
(7) Date of publication. In the case of sociology it seems that the second
World War brought with it great reevaluations. We can for example
draw a line at 1945, and then deal with ten-year intervals. We could
try the following scale:

1. Published in 1935 or earlier.
2. Published 1936–1945.
3. Published 1946–1955.
4. Published 1956–1965.
5. Published later than 1965.

The publication values' interaction with one another

We imagine that the most esteemed forms of publication make the great-
est demands on the contribution's scientific value total, bring out the
strongest limitation of the number of pages, and are least inclined to
admit names of authors low down on the scale. We also expect his
scientific value totals to raise the number of pages allowed, and to be
found more often among the more distinguished authors. Lastly, the
distinguished authors should also be allowed a larger number of pages.

The publications from the well-known universities are included in
greater numbers in the esteemed periodicals or series, come from higher
value totals on average, in larger numbers of pages and with more distinguished authors. We cannot include the publications' academic subjects in this discussion, and we leave them out. If we concentrate on
the *publication* and ignore the *publishing*, the date of publication should
finally be positively correlated with the value total (which is of course
a modern total value), with the form of publication, with the value of
the author's name, and with the seat of learning, since all these variables
are graded according to the current situation.

We thus expect an interaction of the unified value pattern type, which
is what we should expect seeing that the sample of publications includes
all of them, from top publications down to the bottom.

We can summarize the correlations which we expect in a matrix,
Table 22.

We have only one minus sign in the matrix. We have expected that
the more esteemed the publication form, the fewer the number of pages
allowed in the contribution. This however applies only to the periodicals,

Table 22. *Expected matrix for the publication grades' correlations with each other and with certain background variables*

No.	Variable	1	2	3	4	5	7
1	Reputation of the publication form	× ×	+	−	+	+	+
2	Scientific value total	+	× ×	+	±	+	+
3	Number of pages in the work	−	+	× ×	+	+	?
4	Value of the author's name	+	±	+	× ×	+	+
5	Seat of learning of the author	+	+	+	+	× ×	+
7	Date of publication	+	+	?	+	+	× ×

not to the bookseries, and clearly reflects the situation in the periodicals market, where the two variables tend to compensate for each other. We can of course try to get rid of this minus sign but it is simplest to let it stand and bear in mind the circumstances behind it. The publication values' grades follow one another otherwise, and even include the seat of learning's grade. The date has positive correlations of course, since we have given present day values preference, except in the case of the number of pages.

A more ambitious presentation with a division of the sample

We would have a greater chance of finding compensation patterns if we limited the samples so that they were rendered more homogeneous. We can achieve this in a number of ways: according to periodical, country, seat of learning, date or subjects. We must also include more differentiated views of the essays, and will achieve this most simply by removing the value total and including the sixteen scientific values which it constituted, instead. Thus, we still intend to study a wide sample of writings.

The first step in such an analysis is to carry out a survey of how each variable, that we use to split up our sample, is linked with the publication values. We have six such variables to discuss and study:

(1) *How does the degree (or title) of the author affect his writing?*
We can see which scientific values are most dependent on the authors' academic position and how they are affected by it. We can also take a sample of institutions, divide up the members of the staff into categories and then carry out a survey of how the various categories' writings differ.

(2) *How do various types of publications differ?* In the same way we sort out the differences in scientific values between the various levels of publication, partly in our large sample, and partly in publications from a sample of institutions. Which scientific values are taken care of, not only on the reputable levels, but even on the less esteemed levels?

(3) How do the various universities differ? We can for example compare production from similar institutions in Stockholm, Lund, Gothenburg and Uppsala, partly in the large sample and partly in a specially taken sample of all institutions for certain selected subjects. If we include sociology among the latter, we must bear in mind that the scientific values of this book bear the mark of the value system at Stockholm University, which should therefore be promoted in certain respects. Further, the value system of an institution can be better suited to one periodical rather than another.

(4) *How do the various dates of publication differ?* It is in fact far too difficult to even sketch this. The subjects arrive, disappear or are altered, likewise countries, universities, publication series and publication forms, not merely the scientific values. We can possibly pick out one or two easily accessible supplementary problems: how have publications from a couple of ancient institutions, which are still going strong, been altered? How have a couple of long established periodicals, preferably at the top (as for example the *American Sociological Review* which has more than 30 years behind it) altered their value systems? It sounds simpler than it is, but we have already discussed this particular problem earlier.

(5) *How do the various subjects differ?* Each subject usually attaches particular importance to a number of values, more or less connected to material or methods which are often of use within the subject. But it is presumably just as difficult to point out the obvious and joint scientific values as to find those which are specific for the subject.

The subjects do not differ only in scientific values however, but also in the level of their authors, the average can vary for scientific value totals also, as well as publication level, number of pages, etc. We can either take a sample of institutions, or a sample of periodicals of high class, but if such comparisons are to achieve anything, we must have usable lists of scientific values. We do not possess these and do not seem to have much chance of making any for some time. But, we can of course carry out test investigations and see in which direction they point.

(6) *How would an investigation at the highest level of ambition look?* We would clearly take very limited samples of publications, definite

136

categories of authors, types of publication, seats of learning, countries, dates and subjects. We would also have a large and well worked out presentation of variables. But we have in fact already laid out this investigation previously. In that case we intended to study the interaction between the scientific values in a sample of scientific works and we also linked certain publication variables with the scientific values. We are now trying to study the interaction between publication values, and we include among these a large number of scientific values.

The difference between the investigations thus comes from the fact that we have removed some scientific values which are hard to measure in the list of variables for the publication investigation, and have included a number of new ones: the reputation of the publication form, the author's university subject, and date of publication. We have of course, just as much use for these extra categories when we study the scientific values' interaction, and we have in fact thought of using them when we limit population and sample.

The author, the publisher and the reader

To publish as much as possible at as high a level as possible is not an end in itself. We hope to be read, to have our theories and results accepted, to make a contribution to the great international research work. The greater the circulation and the more esteemed the publication form, the greater will be the chances of reaching the competent and relevant readership, to be quoted and to be allowed to take part in scientific advances. It is presumably this expected effect upon the readership's researchers which lies behind the majority of our publication variables.

But the author has very limited possibilities of reaching the readership by his own devices. There is no longer any opportunity for all researchers to maintain contact with all other researchers, not even within strictly limited subjects. Researchers are forced to limit literature reading to the most rewarding periodicals and one or other monographs in his particular field. And thus, the periodical's publisher and publishing house come into the picture.

How do they make their selection? In principle, they must of course look after the interests of the readership, which makes the business economically possible. The readership buys those products which it wants. But those scientists who for a time accept the work of looking after a periodical and of judging manuscripts, have of course their value systems which they are unable to ignore. They quite naturally do the same thing as professors: they mark or grade scientific works and attempt to adequately brush up those manuscripts which can nevertheless be accepted.

In principle therefore, we could amuse ourselves by finding out what the publisher's own value profile looks like, and then the affinity between the latter and that of the contributions published. But, we would not get much from this. In the first place we can only gain access to the published articles, not those rejected. Secondly, the contributors presumably have a certain knowledge of the publisher's value system and he will most probably receive a fairly large proportion of contributions marked by the same viewpoint. Thirdly, the publisher is more or less conscious of this selection mechanism and he tries to some extent to compensate for it. He can call in advisors with somewhat different evaluations and if he is afraid that they will be influenced by authors' names, etc., he can cut away identifying data before he sends over the manuscript for remarks. Fourthly, his subjective selection is countered by "special editions", devoted to a current problem, in which somewhat deviating essays creep in, as long as they are concerned with the correct problem.

CHAPTER 13

Summary

(1) Universities are given more prestige the larger they are, the greater budget they have, and this prestige of size reflects on the president, who has achieved to raise his university by producing the support from the faculty and politicians. But at the same time there operates also an egalitarianism, upward, not downward; making aspiring universities believe that with time and appropriate funding, they may approach the stature of leading institutions.

(2) With the expansion of population and/or education this wish for growth can be fulfilled at the undergraduate level easily. The expansion is really important on the graduate level. This change has of course affected the value orientation of the faculties. Good teaching at undergraduate level is no longer a merit, compared to research and writing, as they bring with them not only publicity but also attention to the university and grants used to increase graduate enrollments.

(3) The academic man is ranked not only on the position list from instructor to full professor, chairman, dean and president but also on his role performance as researcher, administrator, teacher, etc., although top positions are exclusively administrative roles. The role of researcher all the same seems to give more status than the role of administrator at least in the middle positions, and far more status than the teacher.

(4) The academic tries to take the role best suited to his interests and capacity and tries to maximize his benefits. This of course creates role conflicts. Faculty members incompetent for or uninterested in research work are by subtle pressures forced to try. Good teachers are given little recognition, etc. For the moment there is a tendency to respect student's grievances and press for teaching.

(5) These role conflicts are generally not conscious and practically never studied or handled the way sociologists are supposed to study role expectations, role conflicts or even role systems of institutions. Sociologists seldom use sociology for their own use. If sociologists look at the few relevant sociological books on the problems of sociologists in their society

and at the meager interest in them, we sociologists "learn from sociology that we do not learn from sociology".

(6) Grants are important to the research of the universities and so some universities organize bureaus of projects to inform about funds, etc., and to assist in the application process. The bureau gets status in proportion to the amount of research money and grants it brings in.

(7) The bureau seeks out funding agencies and appropriate faculty for available projects, which might influence research policy, especially when the bureau knows what problems and methods the granting agency favors or says it favors.

(8) The pursuit of funds for research might make the bureau—and the faculty—less careful in examining and evaluating the granting agency's requirements and interests, such as involvement in the internal affairs of another society.

(9) The pressure for research is, however, strong enough in itself. Problems that can attract financial support are desperately sought after. Some of these problems cannot be researched, some contribute very little to theories, methods and facts.

(10) A large grant to a researcher gives him not only status but also power. He can ask for promotion, raise of salary, etc., because other universities would be anxious to take over him and his grant. This pattern of pressing the administration is, however, a general tendency and probably goes back to the time when the academic administration had many anxious candidates applying for posts and then used the opportunity to press them.

(11) The grants from foundations and government agencies not only bring with them a tendency toward the problems, methods and solutions valued by them, the grants also make the universities vulnerable and unwilling to criticize federal and state funding agencies, even if they make unreasonable demands on the researcher.

(12) The professional over involvement with research might lead to disinterest in the student and neglect of teaching. This could be one reason for student rebellion.

(13) The role of researcher and writer thus has high status, but is hazardous and replete with difficulties. The literature in the field generally is enormous, which means that it takes a tremendous amount of time to develop proposals, research designs and contacts with foundations and agencies. Those at last rescued from this press by a grant, are instead pressed for results. The project might be difficult, results may be inconclusive, some one else may have published something very similar.

140

The role of researcher requires dedication, discipline and luck. Conflicts may be intensive.

(14) The role of teacher may be initially satisfactory, but likely to turn sour when rewards are not forthcoming and difficulties to follow the literature and to adapt to the attitude of students steadily growing. Some teachers remain at larger institutions although poorly paid and slowly advanced and thus resentful, resisting the general trend, feeling trapped and rejected. Or they might gravitate toward smaller and lesser known institutions where the pressure to engage in research and writing is weak.

(15) The role of administrator may satisfy many of the faculty members' requirements of status without pressures to engage in research, as the roles of chairman, dean, vice-president and president possess legitimate power over others, over researchers, their salaries, promotions and working conditions. The rapid expansion of higher education has brought with it a still more rapid expansion of administration, which has functioned as a safety valve, trying and accepting faculty members, who have moved into administration in search of power. Still this transfer or promotion may not solve their conflicts. Many administrators make apologies for not being able to do research.

(16) Administrators, recruited from those dissatisfied with their previous roles, easily accept the view of watch-dogs of public interest, see that taxpayers' money is properly spent and teaching loads at a maximum, which often is a cloak for hidden anti-intellectualism and hostility to change. But the administrator has to pay for his power, has to use it so as to reward those who support him. The chairman has to please the majority of his faculty and his dean; the dean must please the majority of the chairmen and his vice-president and so on. This can prove extremely difficult, force the administrator to act or change as little as possible. His hope then is to move to another administrative position, as he probably neither is able to take up the researcher role again, nor anxious to return to teaching at a reduced salary.

(17) University administrators are indispensable as leaders of the academic community. They are recruited from all kinds of faculty members, not exclusively from those unable to adapt to their roles. Administrators are sometimes able to make their role personally rewarding and socially productive.

(18) The faculty members who seek administrative roles make themselves available with services and information without threatening those above or the administrative pattern. Moving too fast, criticizing too much, tends to disqualify a candidate. Such a rejected candidate often turns against

the administration and assumes the role of spokesman for the faculty, often providing constructive opposition.

(19) In many American universities, the administration functions with a managerial ideology, placing emphasis on order, accommodation, and efficiency. Both the administration and the faculty have value premises of their own and each may be involved in a struggle for power.

(20 We have tried to show, that role behaviors as researcher, administrator, teacher, faculty spokesman or just good fellow in the faculty tend to exclude each other, as the researcher does not care for other roles, the administrator generally has had to give up research work and does not find rewards in teaching, the teacher neither can research, nor administer, the faculty spokesman finds this reward, because no other is at his disposal and the good fellow probably will turn sour in the long run and secure a position outside the university. We suggest this could be studied empirically with simple scales for measuring different role behaviors.

(21) We could try to measure researcher role behaviors or rather their rewards with a) research publications, b) received grants, c) honorary scientific posts, to measure administrative rewards in d) committeeship and e) administrative promotion, teachers' role rewards with f) number of students in courses and g) published textbooks (a very debatable measure). The reward of the faculty spokesman is not easy to measure, but we suggest h) articles in dailies. And then the reward to the good fellow might be i) obtaining a position outside the university.

(22) If we were able to use these scales on a sample of departments to measure the rewards given to their faculty members during five years, we would expect the role rewards a, b, and c to form a cluster, positively correlated with each other, but negatively correlated with d, e, f, g, h, i. The rewards d and e in the same way should correlate with each other positively but negatively with the values a, b, c, g, h, and i. Rewards f and g should show the same pattern. Reward h should be negatively correlated with all other variables and so should i.

(23) These correlations could be brought together in a matrix, showing the interaction pattern between the different role behaviors and rewards, suggesting if and how they are able to compensate lack of each other. We could try to measure their importance to the faculty in two different ways: we could try to find a general criterion such as status in faculty and use this to correlate with each role or reward behavior. These correlations we use as importance measures and call *criterion importance*. The second possibility we can use is the correlations with variables in other

clusters. The stronger negative correlations, the easier this variable has to compensate the lack in other variables and the more importance it should have. We thus can use the mean of the negative correlations with variables in other clusters as measures of importance and call them *interaction weights*. These measures can only give the rank order of the variables' importance, and their rank order according to criterion importance should be about the same as that according to interaction weights, provided that the variables were valued the same way by the faculty members in the sample.

(24) The researcher's role can be studied with content analysis of his writings where he strives to attain a number of scientific values, such as hypotheses formulated in advance, reliability, validity, representativeness, usefulness for society, etc., correct treatment of data, relevant literature covered, etc. These values we divide in three groups: *planning values* which are brought in during the planning of the project, *working values* which come into play during the research work and *additional values,* coming in at the completion of the work.

(25) Already when planning the project the researcher has to allocate his resources between different scientific values, which then should compete or compensate for each other. If we study this interaction of values in a sample of dissertations, we can measure for each value the grade it has attained. These grades should form clusters of positively correlated variables, but have negative correlations with variables belonging to other (that is, competing) clusters. We call this pattern the *Compensation pattern.*

(26) The sample strongly influences the type of interaction shown in the matrix. If our sample includes scientific writings of all kinds, there would be a number of ambitious dissertations taking good care of many scientific values and also a number of very bad articles, with low grades. This would tend to give positive correlations between the grades of all values, just one cluster containing all values. We call that pattern *the unified value* pattern. If, however, our sample was chosen so, that all the publications had had about the same research resources, they would vary rather little in scientific effort but instead in the direction of this effort. Then we expect a matrix with clearcut clusters, the values correlated positively with values in the same cluster and negatively with values in competing clusters. If our sample is somewhere in the middle between these two extremes, the two tendencies (positive correlations *between* classes of publications, negative correlations *within* classes) would neutralize each other and give a matrix with some clusters of positively corre-

lated variables but very low correlations between variables from different clusters. We call this the *compromise* pattern.

(27) Researchers are not only forced to allocate their resources when planning a project. When the project is under way and data are coming in, these data often do not fullfill their expectations and then they are forced to reevaluate their situation and to reallocate their resources, so as to some extent compensate the grades they have lost. Planning values can seldom be used this way, as they already have been pressed to the utmost in the planning stage, but working values can and then in the last round also additional values. We thus expect the clusters of planning values to take in most or all of the working values, while the remaining working values and the additional values form clusters of their own, used to compensate at the last moment for losses in other values.

(28) We thus expect compensation pattern to show in the interaction of values as it appears in matrices of value grades' correlations, if we select a sample of publications, having had similar research resources. We have tried this hypothesis in four samples: Swedish doctors' dissertations in Sociology, M.A. theses from the Sociological department of Stockholm university, articles from one year of *American Sociological Review* and articles from three volumes of *Acta Sociologica*. All four samples can be said to show a compensation pattern. The resulting clusters have the same main composition: one very large cluster containing most planning and working values connected with empirical research (the empirical cluster), one large cluster containing values connected with theoretical research (the theoretical cluster) and several small clusters dominated by additional values.

(29) An analysis of the interaction pattern of values in the sample of Ph.D. theses shows that there is a unique cluster in this sample, not found in the three others containing the three values sampling, social usefulness and large materials, indicating that these dissertations often investigate important social or administrative problems. The corresponding analysis of the interaction pattern of values in the sample of M.A. theses reveals the strategy of M.A. candidates presenting their theses. If it is dangerously low in scientific grades, their first defence is to use our own summation theory and to write many pages, their second to try giving additional information (that nobody has asked for) and have the theses translated into a foreign language, the third is to cite more than 100 references and try to keep the worst deficiences hidden in the text.

(30) We have tried to measure the importance of the values, that is, to rank them according to criterion importance and interaction weight.

As criterion for Ph.D. dissertations we used their mark, given by the faculties and for M.A. theses the mark given by the professor (Boalt). As criterion for the articles we tried the totals of value grades, which can be used as the theses samples showed that it was correlated with the marks. When we compare all four samples we thus used the criterion importance with grade sum as criterion. The importance can be analyzed only in the empirical cluster and with the criterion importance, the interaction weights varying too much. Three values seem to possess great importance: no. 16, statistical model, value 14, definitions, and value 18, actuality of scales. Three values seem to have little importance: value 11, usefulness to society, no. 12, news value, and no. 21, size of material.

(31) We expected, that if one sample of researchers placed a special value in another cluster than the other samples, that was an indication that they paid more or less attention to it than the others. This should show on the grade mean of the sample, that then was higher or lower than was expected. But what mean to expect? Well, we know that the total grade sum is highest in the Ph.D. sample, goes down in the M.A. sample, still lower in the sample for *American Sociological Review* and lowest in the sample from *Acta Sociologica*. This sinking tendency should show up for the values placed in the empirical cluster by all four samples, but it should be broken for the values not unanimously placed in the empirical cluster. The test proved this to be true, and we thus believe that different samples of researchers not only have different sets of scientific values, but also that they might pay them more or less attention and at the same time place them in different contexts. And if a sample pays more or less attention to a grade than other samples, this evidently should show also in criterion importance and interaction weights, which hypotheses were supported, or rather, not rejected by test.

(32) How does the researcher acquire his scientific values? On the American Academic Market place the competent students ask some university departments for bids and take the best. But then they are up to a point tied to the scientific value system of the professor in charge of the research or the teaching they are to assist with. This, however, by no means makes it impossible or even difficult to get another adviser, another problem to handle in the dissertation or to rely more on the other members of the committee. This amount of freedom contrasts with the situation in European universities: The student there can choose university and department, but nothing more. There is one single professor in the field, one problem area, one method and one technique to transfer the professor's values as intact as possible to the student.

(33) The American universities probably once showed the same tendencies but the educational boom: more universities, more departments, more students in the departments, more faculty, more competition about competent faculty members and more administrative work for the chairman brought about the present system. European universities are probably slowly following the same trend, changing in many respects but six seem to be more important: 1) The size of the department and its faculty grows, 2) more and more fields of research are covered by the faculty, 3) all researchers have more status and salary, not only full professors, 4) the researchers can move from one university to another, 5) the chairman of the department gets more involved in administration, 6) students have more freedom of choice and are less dependent of their professors. But this freedom for researchers and students at the same time breaks up the old security of the universities, where an examination, a qualified work and high status was in practice guaranteed to everybody staying faithfully with his professor, learning the right set of values and the right kind of literature. That security is gone and you can get no more on the Academic Market than your work entitles you to.

(34) The chairman and the famous researcher are no longer identities, as the researcher often does not want to be tied down with administration. He generally prefers to build his personal empire, using his publications and grants to press for a salary raise, to press for larger grants and for status in his scientific associations. An empire builder need not counteract his chairman, his dean, his foundation contacts, his association fellow brethren, etc., as they in one sense are building their empires too—and could include his empire too. The good empire builders may get on very well with each other, exchanging services and status. The good researcher thus might build a personal empire: use his good publications to raise his salary, his status and achieve large grants in order to publish more material, etc. In practice this circle cannot go on indefinitely as the good researcher turning into a successful empire builder no longer is able to remain a good researcher—and certainly no longer able to transmit scientific values to graduate students. He might, however, turn to administration.

(35) We suggest that the career pattern of the scientific empire builder can be studied in *American Men of Science* and *Who's Who in America*. A sample of successful scientific empire builders can be taken by including in it for instance only academicians from the Behavioral Sciences (or may be only sociologists) having attained the status of *Who's Who in America*. Using the two biographical directories, we could list for them

146

1) academic performance, 2) faculty positions, 3) honorary posts in associations, 4) interaction with foundations, 5) interaction with scientific councils, 6) assignments from state or federal government agencies, 7) military assignments and 8) publications mentioned in the directories (other sources could be used too). These data would be used in several ways to find out if these rewards have to be reaped in a certain sequence or if one cluster of rewards can compensate for the lack of another or if it is just the number of rewards that make it possible to have more rewards.

(36) We now turn to the departments. They are meant to attract as good students as possible, to make them take good grades, to attract teachers and researchers, give them resources, help them to grants and publication. All these points can be handled as the values of the departments and it is possible to apply our usual techniques here: take a sample of departments, measure their grades on the different value scales, compute the correlations between the various value grades and then present all these intercorrelations in a matrix. But the interaction pattern of this matrix depends on the sample. If the sample is representative of all American university departments, the big departments will have everything and the small departments very little of anything. Such a sample evidently must show a unified value pattern: all intercorrelations between the value grades are positive. If we take a sample where these large or very small departments are excluded, we expect the compromise pattern, that is, very low correlations between the grades. Eventually, if we take a sample of similar departments of about the same size and/or resources, it might happen that they tend to use these resources in different ways, allocating more to theoretical research, theory, etc., or to empirical data collection or to teaching, etc. Then this could show as a compensation pattern in the matrix.

(37) We have to add that our technique probably is of much less use for the study of departments than for the study of researchers or research reports. The researcher alone makes his decisions, the department is an organization and the decisions are made by different persons who might disagree on important points. The researcher has limited resources and must allocate them very carefully, the department has larger resources, but often more or less earmarked for special purposes. The allocation process probably gives less information on the department level. The researcher has been trained to pay respect to his scientific values, but there is no similar training of department personnel to take care of department values. Still a department is a communicating group

and should attain some kind of consensus on department values. Maybe this consensus is strong enough to make it visible through the veils of the matrices.

(38) We have discussed the researcher's role (work on his own project), the research group member's role (working on the project of the group) and the role of empire builder. These three roles can easily overlap, but there is also the risk for conflicts between them. We have tried to analyse the three types of conflicts and then apply Goode's theory of role strain for the most interesting type of conflict, that between the role of researcher and the role of empire builder.

(39) We have been careful to restrict our set of scientific roles to the usual and non-controversial values. We thus avoid in the first place all such as political opinion, ideas about the society's real needs, etc. In the second place we try to escape the controversial scientific values just by ignoring them. We have for instance not tried to include the scientific values characteristic for Marx or even for Weber in our set. We have to admit this weakness. Since there is yet no list of scientific values important to present day sociologists published, we see for the moment no easy way out of this dilemma. The sociologist should at least be conscious of this problem.

(40) The researcher's role probably collides to some degree with all his other roles. This could be studied by using *Who's Who in America* once more to compare scientists mentioned there with other successful citizens in the United States. We expect the scientists to have a lower proportion married, to marry later, to have fewer children, to have less assignments for federal or state government, have a lower proportion mentioning club membership, sons or daughters of the American Revolution, churchmembership, masonic orders, etc.

(41) We expect thus the scientists to show signs of a withdrawal from the roles of everyday life. They are to some extent alienated from it and so able to look at it with a critical eye and maybe the eye is extra critical looking at the top men of everyday life: big businessmen, great politicians, top ranking soldiers, influential clergymen, etc. But then the scientists instead are much more engaged in science and research—being little interested in analysing the role of the scientist. They are too close to this problem.

(42) Can we use the technique for analysing the problems of the Academic Market place to study other sections of society? We have tried to show that the same technique we use to describe the Academic Market place (departments, faculty members and students all bidding and select-

ing one another and at the same time accepting or selling scientific values) can be used to describe the Marriage Market Place, men and women bidding and selecting one another and at the same time accepting or selling family values. This problem actually is better adapted to our technique, as men and women seem to evaluate one another on the same scales, while scientists have to use one set for departments, another for faculty members or graduate students.

(43) The interaction within the family can be studied along the same lines as the departments. A family should produce children, educate them, see them through a good school, provide a reasonable income and allocate some of it to a reasonable living place, invest money in the cultural tools, as books, music instruments, remain without contacts with social relief agencies and stay out of prison. If we take a sample of families, we should find that so many of them come out so well on these scales—and another, smaller number with many children come out badly, with low grades. We thus expect that a representative sample would give us a matrix of correlations showing a unified value pattern. We have demonstrated this on a Swedish sample. But if we choose a sample of families of restricted means we should be able to show a compensation pattern matrix, as they have small resources and must allocate them carefully according to their main values, children, car, standard of living—may be even research.

(44) We turn our interest to the publication market and try to apply the summation theory there. Which values are important to the scientific publication consumer? We suggest that he prefers well-known publication series to unknown, scientific valuable contributions to the less valuable, many pages to few (unless he has to read them), publications from well known universities to those from little known, those from esteemed fields of research to those from less esteemed fields and recent publications to out-moded ones. We suggest scales for those values and expect them to have positive correlations with the grades of one another (with one single exception: top journals will not give a large number of pages to their articles, on the contrary). This is what the summation theory should make likely from the start: a sample containing all kind of publications, from top work to the bottom, of course, should turn out results corresponding to the unified value pattern, that is, positive correlations between all value grades.

(45) We then have sketched somewhat more ambitious studies to find out differences in publication values between various types of authors, types of publications, universities, periods of time and subjects.

(46) We have presented a point of view on the research process and have used the same technique on nearly all our problems. This does not mean that we consider other points of view wrong or unnecessary or other methods inferior.

Appendix

Scales for 29 scientific variables and 3 additional scales.

I. Scales for measurement of *planning values* measurable already in the investigation plan.

(1) *Presentation of the hypotheses*
1. Investigation not intended to test or present hypotheses.
2. Hypotheses not discussed, all implicit.
3. Hypotheses discussed, but not statistically precise.
4. Hypotheses statistically precise by a previously given significance level, none of them deduced.
5. Some hypotheses deduced.

Reliability .88.

(2) *Reliability in methods of measurement*
1. Reliability impossible to measure or estimate.
2. Reliabilities probably low (among other things, low prediction capacity).
3. Reliabilities not measured, but probably high (i.e. register data).
4. Reliabilities for certain main variables on average below .50.
5. Reliabilities for certain main variables on average over .50.

Reliability .56.

(3) *Validity of dependent or independent variables, one or some of them*
1. Prediction validity not measured, logical validity not discussed.
2. Prediction validity is not measured, logical validity discussed in less than 3 lines.
3. Prediction validity not measured, logical validity discussed in three lines or more.
4. Prediction validity for certain variables given, the mean below .50.
5. Prediction validity for certain main variables given, the mean above .50.

Reliability .74.

(4) *Selection of sample*
   1. Sample contains grave errors.
   3. Sample contains small errors.
   5. Sample correct.
Reliability .72.

(5) *Generalization of the situation*
   1. Generalization not discussed.
   3. Generalization discussed, but in less than 3 lines.
   5. Generalization discussed, in 3 lines or more.
Reliability .73.

(6) *Integration of the problem*
   1. Problem isolated, not connected to theory.
   2. Problem isolated, secondary connection to theory which is of little importance.
   3. Problem of about equal importance as the theory used.
   4. Problem of some interest, but theory of more interest.
   5. Problem involves only testing of a theory.
Reliability .57.

(7) *Investigation's value for theory construction in general*
   1. Value neither implied nor asserted.
   3. Value implied, not asserted.
   5. Value asserted.
Reliability 1.00.

(8) *Investigation's value for hypotheses formation in general*
   1. Value neither implied nor asserted.
   3. Value implied, not asserted.
   5. Value asserted.
Reliability .98.

(9) *Investigation's value for statistical model formation in general*
   1. Value neither implied nor asserted.
   3. Value implied, not asserted.
   5. Value asserted.
Reliability .98.

(10) *Investigation's value for variable construction in general*
   1. Value neither implied nor asserted.

152

3. Value implied, not asserted.
5. Value asserted.

Reliability 1.00.

(11) *Investigation's usefulness to society*
1. Social use neither suggested nor implied.
2. Social use suggested with frequency data, importance, or implied.
3. Social use named, not emphasised, or investigation financed by other organ than research council, community or state authority.
4. Social use named, emphasised with phrases, or investigation ordered by community or state authority.
5. Social use supported by numerical calculations or implied through official assignment.

Reliability .67.

(12) *Problem's news value*
1. Problem same as before, tested with same methods.
2. Problem enlargement of previous method *partly* altered.
3. Problem linked with previous, but largely new. Method *partly* altered.
4. Problem new, only slight connections. Largely older methods.
5. Problem new, largely new methods.

Reliability .29.

(13) *Research school's usefulness*
1. Problem not within chairman's framework, neither presented as such.
2. Problem not within chairman's framework, yet presented as such.
3. Problem within chairman's framework, yet not presented as such.
4. Problem within chairman's framework and presented as such.
5. Problem to defend own research school on broad front.

Reliability .82.

II. Scales for the measurement of *working values,* which come into play during research work.

(14) *Variables' definition*
1. Main variables not operationally defined.
2. Certain main variables operationally defined, the others not defined.

3. All main variables operationally defined, explicitly or implicitly.
4. All main variables operationally defined, but not nominally.
5. All main variables defined both operationally and nominally.

Reliability .76.

(15) *Mathematical model*

1. No discussion.
2. Verbal discussion.
3. Explicit first grade equation. Formula.
4. Explicit high-grade equation. Formula.
5. Derivative.
6. Integral.

Reliability .96.

(16) *Statistical aspect*

1. No model.
2. Model neither deterministic nor probabilistic.
3. Model deterministic.
4. Model probabilistic.

Reliability .52.

(17) *Treatment of data with scales*

1. No scales.
2. Only nominal scales.
3. Ordinal scales (Guttman, Osgood), some nominal scales.
4. Interval scales (Thurstone), possibly also some lower scales.
5. Ratio scales, possibly lower scales for certain variables.

Reliability .53.

(18) *Scale's actuality*

1. No scale.
2. Additive scale (Likert type). Certain comparisons in pairs.
3. Thurstone scales.
4. Guttman, Lazarsfeld.
5. Osgood.

Reliability .89.

(19) *Analysis method's value*

1. Method of analysis incorrect.
2. Method of analysis merely routine, without attention paid to the character of data.

154

3. Method of analysis more or less suited to the purpose.
4. Method of analysis refined.
5. Method of analysis new in important respects.

Reliability .66.

(20) *Mathematical treatment of data*

1. No mathematical treatment.
2. Only central tendency and possibly distribution measurement.
3. Correlations, chi², Z- or t-test.
4. Variance analysis.
5. Factor analysis.
6. Matrix mathematics.

Reliability .69.

(21) *Material's size (if more than one, added together)*

1. Under 51 observations.
2. 51–100 observations.
3. 101–300 observations.
4. 301–1000 observations.
5. Over 1000 observations.

Reliability .87.

(22) *Non-response in the material (if more than one, the main material)*

1. Non-response not presented.
2. Non-response over 30 %.
3. Non-response between 15 % and 30 %.
4. Non-response between 5 % and 15 %.
5. Non-response between 2 % and 5 %.
6. Non-response less than 2 %.

Reliability .54.

(23) *Fate of the hypotheses*

1. One half or more of the hypotheses rejected.
2. Between a half and a quarter rejected.
3. Between a quarter and an eighth rejected.
4. Almost all accepted, $p < 0.05$, < 0.01.
5. Almost all accepted, $p < 0.01$.

Reliability .50.

III. Scales for the measurement of *additional values,* which are introduced in the last phase of the work.

(24) *Information additional to planned report*

1. No information added to planned report.
2. Neither new hypotheses nor variables, but continued investigations discussed more than 3 lines.
3. Assisting hypotheses discussed, but no new variables introduced.
4. Assisting hypotheses tested, but new variables not introduced.
5. New variables introduced.

Reliability .04. The scale then revised to the form given above, but not possible to obtain independent estimation and so the reliability not known.

(25) *Passage through literature*

1. No literature cited.
2. 1–5 sources cited.
3. 6–10 sources cited.
4. 11–25 sources cited.
5. 26–50 sources cited.
6. 51–100 sources cited.
7. 101–200 sources cited.
8. More then 200 sources cited.

Reliability .89.

(26) *Language (from the Swedish point of view)*

1. Swedish, from start to end.
2. Swedish, but with foreign language summary.
3. Language other than Swedish, German, English or French.
4. English, German or French. Technical words translated badly.
5. English, German or French. Technical words well translated. Dull style.
6. English, German or French. Technical words well translated. Good style.

Reliability .98.

(27) *Number of pages in the publication. Large pages multiplied by two*

1. 10 pages or more.
2. 11–25 pages.
3. 26–50 pages.
4. 51–99 pages.
5. 100–150 pages.
6. 151–250 pages.

7. 251–500 pages.

8. More than 500 pages.

Reliability .99.

(28) *Value of researcher's title (degree)*

1. Neither master, nor assistant teacher.

2. Master, doctor or assistant teacher.

3. Instructor, research fellow or assistant professor.

4. Associate professor.

5. Full professor.

Reliability not tested, as all the 21 authors of the theses by definition must be masters and thus belong to grade 2, or in some cases 3.

(29) *Presentation's ability to disguise the deficiencies of the project*

1. None.

2. Slight.

3. Moderate.

4. Considerable.

5. Very high.

Reliability .61.

IV. Scales for measuring *year of publication, mark received on theses* and *sum of scientific value grades on scales 1–29.*

(30) *Year of publication.* The first Swedish thesis in sociology came 1947 and we made this study end of 1966. We thus get the following classes

1. 1947–50

2. 1951–54

3. 1955–58

4. 1959–62

5. 1963–66

(31) *Mark given by the faculty to the theses, according to the seven steps used by Swedish faculties*

1–7

(32) *Sum of scientific value grades on scales 1–29 listed above*

1–5